BECOMING A WOMAN WHO KNOWS GOD BY NAME

JAN HARRISON

HARVEST HOUSE PUBLISHERS
EUGENE, OREGON

Cover by Rightly Designed, Buckley, Washington

BECOMING A WOMAN WHO KNOWS GOD BY NAME
Copyright © 2016 Jan Harrison
Published by Harvest House Publishers
Eugene, Oregon 97402
www.harvesthousepublishers.com

ISBN 978-0-7369-6140-0 (pbk.)
ISBN 978-0-7369-6141-7 (eBook)

Printed in the United States of America

16 17 18 19 20 21 22 23 24 / BP-GL / 10 9 8 7 6 5 4 3 2 1

To the faithful group of women in the 2011–2012 Women of the Word Bible Study at Central Church in Charlotte, North Carolina. You helped me stand with a broken heart and a crushed spirit. You allowed me to lead, and you shared my burdens during the darkest storm in my life. Glory to God for using you to guide me to my safe haven.

Then they are glad because they are quiet;
So He guides them to their desired haven.
Psalm 107:30 NKJV

Contents

Those who know Your name will put their trust in You;
For You, Lord, have not forsaken those who seek You.
Psalm 9:10 nkjv

Bless His Holy Name

The decision to know God wholly and personally is one of the most amazing and powerful decisions that you and I can ever embrace. The journey we start today will inspire us to bless His holy name and lead us to be blessed by His names in life-changing ways. The closer we draw to His character, the more we will trust the Lord with every part of our lives and ourselves.

Trust. Trust is at the heart of why we desperately long to know God and why we struggle to know God. If we look at our human relationships, this statement makes more sense. Think about how trust makes or breaks our ties to other people. Our spouses. Our parents. Our extended family members. Our friends. Our leaders. Our coworkers and peers. The sharp point of mistrust drives a wedge between us that keeps us from unity with one another.

It is common for people to openly confess that they have trust issues. Maybe you have heard someone say, "If you had experienced some of the things that I have experienced in my life, you would have trust issues too." Maybe you have even been that person.

So often these trust issues stem from a marked moment in time or recurring incidents when someone close to us fails us in some way. Sometimes that person has completely misrepresented who they are and they have broken the trust and violated their end of the relationship. And sometimes it's because you and I have misplaced expectations on a relationship or on a person.

No wonder we desire to be able to fully trust our creator and Lord. We want—no, we need—to lean into Him and learn who He says He is. But, my friend, maybe there have been times when you have been uncertain whether you know God completely. Maybe you have challenged His faithfulness during a heartbreaking time in your life.

If you are honest with yourself and Him, you might say today, "The truth of the matter is, Lord, things have not really turned out in my life the way I thought they would or the way I thought they should. I deserved for things to work out differently than they have."

In our dark hours, maybe you and I have cried to God out of frustration, "I'm disappointed, Lord. You let me down. I never really expected for my life to look the way it looks, for the people who have broken relationships with me to do the things that they've done. Lord, where were You and where are You now? I prayed, I asked, I believed, I stood. What happened? Did You abandon me?"

At the root of each of those questions and thoughts, if we're honest, is a distrust of the Lord. That's difficult to admit. Who wants to say they don't trust the God of the universe? Yet over time and through various situations, it could be that you have lessened your dependence on Him. Maybe you have questioned His ways during a season of life and never felt safe to trust Him with all of your heart and your decisions after that. Have your circumstances undermined your faith in God's faithfulness? Numbers 23:19 provides us with an important perspective: "God is not a man, that He should lie, nor a son of man, that He should repent. Has He said, and will He not do? Or has He spoken, and will He not make it good?" (NKJV). When we feel broken or disheartened, we forget that God is not a person like us, muddling along. He is the Almighty. God is right beside us in our pain, and He is the one with the plan.

God is who He says He is and does what He says He will do. He cannot lie. He makes no mistakes. He never exploits you for His benefit. He has nothing ever to repent of and He owes us no apologies. Our faithful God will always follow through on His word. He will make good on His promises. It's His character to fulfill His word absolutely and completely. Trust is never misplaced when you trust the Lord.

So if we know that He is absolutely trustworthy, then it is our responsibility and privilege to grow in our trust of Him. This takes time and investment in relationship so we can discover who He is, who He says He is, and how we can rest in the truth of His nature and character. He will show Himself to be faithful. This I know! We will discover His character as we become familiar with His names and call on Him with complete trust in His presence and response.

The Invitation to Trust the Lord

David, the writer of the Psalms, was called "a man after God's own heart" in Scripture, and he was very familiar with trust issues in his relationships with others and also with God. Yet he longed for God's comfort and sought it over and over. Many of his psalms record the struggles and the disappointments, the doubts and the fears, and all the challenges that are a part of relationships; but they also record testimony time and again that God is true to His word and His people. And what leads us to trust, according to David? "Those who know Your name will put their trust in You, for You, O LORD, have not forsaken those who seek You" (Psalm 9:10).

As we explore His names, we must make

> After we have accepted Christ, the most incredible invitation of our faith journey is to know Him and to put our trust in Him.

our hearts and ourselves available. We allow His spirit to teach us about His character and give revelation knowledge to us. This establishes a trust-based relationship. Together you and I are invited to know some of His names intimately, to speak them personally, and to keep growing and maturing in our understanding of God's nature. It is an ongoing pursuit that will deepen our faith beyond what we've known before.

When we accept God's invitation to know Him, there isn't a guarantee that we will understand Him. There will be times when we don't understand the divine decisions of God. My only son, James, died after becoming sick while living and serving in Africa. My family was heartbroken. There were many times when the weight of sorrow and depth of loss was more than I could bear. During this time I learned to lean on the unfailing character of God as never before. He was the only one who could give me strength and fill me with faith to trust Him. His personal care and comfort were revealed to me when I called on His name.

Even in our darkest moments, we can rest in His names, His character, and His leading. What a gift. To trust God's presence is to accept this invitation and this treasure as you become a woman who knows God by name.

Our Path to Bless and Be Blessed

Scripture abounds with God-breathed inspiration and wisdom. There is plenty that draws us toward Him and compels us to know Him more deeply. To honor the beginning of our journey together, I have chosen Psalm 103 to initiate our steps forward. It is a portion of Scripture that I cherish. In fact, I encourage you to make this psalm a part of your daily life and allow it to become part of who you are. Read it, study it, learn it, pray it, and take it into your innermost being. The first five verses lead us to a place of worship, gratitude, praise, and renewal.

Bless the LORD, O my soul;
And all that is within me, bless His holy name!
Bless the LORD, O my soul,
And forget not all His benefits:

Who forgives all your iniquities,
Who heals all your diseases,
Who redeems your life from destruction,
Who crowns you with lovingkindness and tender mercies,
Who satisfies your mouth with good things,
So that your youth is renewed like the eagle's. (NKJV)

As we walk through these first verses, we will draw inspiration and gain momentum for our journey ahead. They shine a bright light on redemption, restoration, and renewal...all that we long for in our pursuit of trusting God more fully.

Bless the LORD, O my soul; and all that is within me, bless His holy name! Bless the LORD, O my soul. (Psalm 103:1-2 NKJV)

If we needed a reason to embark on this adventure, verses one and two share the why and the way to know God. We will spend time in the presence of His names because this will honor and bless Him. And the way we will do this is with our soul: all that is within us.

Notice that David didn't say, "Bless the Lord, O my mind" as a possible option. Our mind wants to raise questions and red flags, reason things out, understand, and translate things based on our limited terms. Consider how often your mind has overruled a best intention, an absolute truth, or even your claim to one of God's promises. It happens often if we are not careful, and that is not God's best for us.

David also did not say, "Bless the Lord, O my flesh." If we are concerned about our minds, then oh my, let us be more concerned about our flesh, right? If we even took a one-week sampling of our life in the flesh, we would likely see a roller-coaster ride of emotions and needs. Let's face it, our needs and desires for more influence, freedom, beauty, fame, status, wealth, etc. pull us in many directions but never toward the cross.

If you try to live by the mind and flesh alone, you will find yourself dizzy from your circumstances. One moment, you feel high. The next minute, you feel low, lost, unworthy. But your spirit can be at rest with God and remain fixed on His presence. When you create a healthy time of devotion and prayer and stillness before the Lord, your spirit can be in communion with Him. This is when He will begin to reveal the beauty of His holiness and the majesty of His name to you and me.

Your spirit, or inner man, is only satisfied when you stay fixed on the name of our Lord. Rest for a moment on that truth. In the hubbub that we call daily living, know that there is a way for your spirit to be captivated by God, immersed in His presence, and open to His leading, comfort, and the Holy Spirit.

It's a remarkable experience to bless the Lord with all that is within you. Have you ever stopped to tell Him with your mouth what you believe about Him in your heart? His Spirit will witness to your spirit that He is worthy of being blessed and praised. When circumstances might tempt you to believe you've been abandoned, neglected, overlooked, or ignored, His Spirit witnessing to your spirit will remind you: *Oh, His name is holy. No matter what I face, I will bless His name. This is not about my circumstances or my desires. It is about blessing Him because He never changes and He is holy at all times. Bless Him.* "Bless the LORD, O my soul, and all that is within me, bless His holy name."

I have been privileged to witness and learn from the example of people who bless His name with all that is within them when the things of the world around them are uncertain, if not dire. These are people who don't know where their next meal will come from, what they'll wear, eat, or where they'll sleep. They don't know what the next hour may bring. But give them an opportunity to get together, give them an opportunity to lift up the name of the Lord, give them a chance to praise God's name one more time, and you better believe that with everything they've got they will burst forth blessing His name and rejoicing in His name. It's so beautiful, and it's so exciting. When you witness pure praise, you realize that nothing should hold you back from blessing His holy name.

Forget not all His benefits. (Psalm 103:2 NKJV)

Psalm 103 serves as our guide to learn how to rest in and bless God's holy name. In the second verse, the psalmist turns our attention to the importance of remembering the spiritual benefits He gives us. I pause here to point out that these benefits surpass the most impressive benefit package the world could ever offer. Yet how often do our minds quickly bring out a list of grievances, doubts, and needs that await tending instead of a list of blessings and benefits?

With practice and trust, our spirit will quickly reject that negative impulse and lead us, instead, to embrace the truth that God's benefits are plentiful and unchanging because He is always and forever, sovereign Lord over all. In Him, our benefits will always be funded. They will never be rescinded. And you don't have to pay your dues or prove your worthiness to receive God's benefits. The One who died for us, the One who has given us the privilege of becoming benefactors of all that God has, says anybody can qualify for them.

What are those benefits? What blessings give us security in the Lord? Let's gather a remarkable sample from Psalm 103.

Who forgives all your iniquities, who heals all your diseases. (Psalm 103:3 NKJV)

Not long ago I was standing at the side of my son's grave, and I looked at the cross at the head of that grave and said, "What else matters?" Not the length of his life, not the things that he did, not the people he was connected to. What else matters but that all of his sins had been forgiven? Life eternal is the benefit. Jesus said, "I am the resurrection and the life. He who believes in Me, though he may die, he shall live. And whoever lives and believes in Me shall never die" (John 11:25-26 NKJV).

Before we can challenge and ask about iniquities that seem too significant and life-shattering to be included in this benefit, remember that you cannot lose or earn these benefits that are presented to you through Christ. Sin does not exclude us. Jesus died on the cross to include us and our past, present, and future iniquities. All of our iniquities have been put under the blood of Jesus for whoever would believe and apply it. What else matters?

Verse three says He heals all of your diseases. You are healed. No matter the prognosis for your physical body, your wellness is a guaranteed benefit. You and I don't know what our healing will look like, and it might not be the resolution of physical frailty that we long for. In fact, we receive our complete healing at death, when our body is at its most fragile, useless, and destroyed. Not long ago a friend's husband passed away after a grueling battle with cancer. Her response was, "He won the battle. He's healed and in the presence of the Lord." This paradoxical, miraculous exchange is for anyone and everyone who is ready for the kingdom of heaven. The question is: Are you fit for the kingdom? Are your sins forgiven? Have you been washed in the blood?

The body—the flesh—might suffer physical harm, and all of us are in a continual stage of diminishment, but even then we are being healed. "We do not lose heart, but though our outer man is decaying, yet our inner man is being renewed day by day" (2 Corinthians 4:16). Your life need not be consumed with diseases like discouragement, depression, disappointment, and defeat. You needn't struggle to just get through a day. This healing is a benefit that belongs to you and me. Receive it!

Who redeems your life from destruction, who crowns you with lovingkindness and tender mercies. (Psalm 103:4 NKJV)

Jesus has offered us a life free from the consequences that we deserve. And I do not care how good and benevolent, sweet and giving someone is, without Christ they are on a path headed for destruction. I didn't say that; that's not my rule. I didn't make up how all this works. Jesus said, "I am the way, the truth, and the life. No one comes to the Father except through Me" (John 14:6 NKJV). He gives us the way to avoid destruction and to rest in His grace.

Many of us still have times when we strive and struggle because we revert to a mindset of having to earn God's grace. That is wasted energy. And that can lead to a wasted life if we aren't careful and discerning. Carrying the lie that you are unworthy of God's benefits will cause labored steps on a road to destruction. Release the lie and embrace the truth that you are made worthy in God through Christ so that you can walk unencumbered in the way, truth, and life.

Salvation is all we need. What will it take for you, for me, to believe this completely? We don't want to miss out on the life and purpose God intends for each of us. Trust this, my friend: through the cross, God has made the way to avoid destruction. A thriving faith is never about what we do; it is about what He has already done. This is cause to praise and rejoice in your salvation. Amen.

How often do your thoughts turn to rejoicing over your salvation? My prayer is that as we make it a heart practice to draw close to God through His names we will rush to rejoicing. Our spirits should be bursting with gratitude as we consider how God chooses to bestow benefits in addition to salvation. He crowns our life with lovingkindness and mercies. The bounty of God's benefits is never-ending. How has He crowned you? Maybe His lovingkindness has embraced you in the form of encouragement, fellowship, strengthening of the body, or even a conviction of trust in the Lord. Perhaps He's shown you tenderness and care in various ways. Maybe there was a word of inspiration shared by someone or a verse, prayer, or a sense of provision that restored your hope for the day. As you recall your personal list of benefits, let your heart and spirit turn to rejoicing. Remember that "every good thing given and every perfect gift is from above, coming down from the Father of lights, with whom there is no variation or shifting shadow" (James 1:17).

Who satisfies your mouth with good things, so that your youth is renewed like the eagle's. (Psalm 103:5 NKJV)

When we walk with God and bless Him, He satisfies us with good things. This translation uses the word "mouth." Other translations reference that He satisfies your years or your desires with good things. Think about that. If we receive satisfaction from what is good and what is of God, then we won't desire anything else. Those things that destroy us, deplete us, or distort our faith won't even be appealing! When we crave and discern what is good, we trust God's supply for our needs. We know His supply exceeds anything the world can offer, and we long for it. The result is that we are renewed in our innermost being. From a nutrition perspective, we all know that healthier food going in will result in a healthier, stronger body. The same is true for our spirit and our mind: healthy in, healthy out. The fruit of being satisfied by God's goodness is that we will share His love. Our life will become a living testimony. Only someone who knows and trusts God's name for their every need can authentically speak words of hope, life, and comfort into someone else's life. When His lovingkindness is shown through us, His benefits multiply. One such benefit is renewal.

Renewal. Ah. Don't we want that so badly?

Just reading verse five causes me to draw a deep breath and let it out with such hope and want. God refreshes the weary spirit. He doesn't do it for Himself; He does it for you and me. I have firsthand experience with renewal. Before my heart was broken by James's death, I didn't fully understand how God renews and restores life. But after that tragic loss, I had knowledge of His mercies in new ways. With desperation, I sought His face, called on His holy name, and ran into His presence for comfort. A miracle happened in my life, and I know this because I'm here and I'm still praising the Lord with everything I have.

For months after James's passing, if I bumped into someone I hadn't seen in a while, they would take a long look at me with curiosity. I knew what they were thinking: *Why doesn't she look like something the cat dragged in?* They would say, "Oh my, after all you've been through, you look strong." I confess now that I did not often feel strong. The grief journey is devastating, and there is not a quick fix through it. And thank goodness that is the case, because every day that I held my broken heart to God, He was there to receive it and to touch it with assurance of His hope and healing. God did not tell me to get over it. God did not challenge me that I was grieving wrongly over the death of my only son. Instead, God was with me in the pit and in the slow return to life. And beyond. I didn't return to life as usual. Who can or even wants to after a piece of life and family is missing? What is purely astonishing is that I didn't return to energy, strength, or faith as usual either. They were multiplied in power. I don't know how else to explain it.

Oh, God has so renewed my youth. God has renewed my strength, God has renewed my heart. It has nothing to do with "getting over" a broken heart. It has nothing to do with coming out of sadness. It has nothing to do with enduring the emotions that go along with all of the circumstances in my life. It has everything to do with God's benefits. His healing. His promises. And His holy name.

God Himself has never been closer. His witness and His Spirit have never been stronger. His truth has never been more real. I have been renewed by the name of the Lord, and that is all I need. That is all you need. I promise you, even though my promise is not an iota of what matters. God promises, and those promises are a whole different story. They are everything!

Oh, yes, He will satisfy your mouth with good things, and He will renew your youth.

Symptoms of Spiritual Amnesia

God's benefits are too great to forget. Recalling them and trusting them is how you encourage yourself in the Lord and strengthen your soul. It sounds simple to merely remember God's goodness, but you will discover that there's a battle going on over us that can cause spiritual amnesia.

The enemy wants us to forget all of these benefits. In fact, he wants you to base your trust in God on your feelings or your circumstances; he wants you to remember every time you've been disappointed. He celebrates when you hold on to a hurt, sorrow, or prayer that wasn't answered in the way you thought it should be.

When your trust level starts to drop and you sense that your innermost being is starting to doubt if God is really there or that He truly cares, you are forgetting His benefits. That is when you will be inclined to revisit every mistake you ever made, every foolish thing you were ever involved in, every moment of failure. This mental spiral can hold you in a destructive pattern. I'm not just talking about people who don't know the Lord. I'm talking about Christians who forget to rehearse those benefits because the enemy is waging a war for their mind.

You'll never be able to accept the crown of lovingkindness or receive the tender mercies as God's benefits for you because you'll say, "I'm not worthy. That's not for me. God wouldn't do that in my life." You'll fail to recognize the hand of God at work in your life. Another symptom of forgetting is that your mouth will constantly speak of the defeat and the disappointment. Those praises and testimonies God wants to place in your mouth will be crowded out by expressed uncertainty about God and unworthiness of self. You'll always be suspicious of what God is up to, and your words will rehearse doubts to yourself and others.

How many times have you heard people say something along the lines of, "We just don't know what's going to happen next; we just don't know what God is going to do next. This is a bad world we live in, so who can trust what will come?" If we personally get like this, we not only wear ourselves out but we wear out everybody else around us. People will wonder, *Where is the evidence of benefits to being a believer in Jesus Christ?*

His benefits should be evident in your life. The enemy of your soul wants you to live drained, depleted, and defeated, because his ultimate goal is to destroy you. And if he can't take you out completely, he'll destroy your testimony and your witness. He will fill your mind and your mouth with grumbling, complaining, and negative comments that will cause people to go in the opposite direction.

Remember. Remember. Remember. When you turn daily to God in prayer and seek Him through His names, you will not forget His benefits.

The Blessing Cycle

Experiencing God's character in a new and personal way will empower us to share His blessings and benefits. Our desire to proclaim His goodness will rise up in us because we know it will bless Him. In that sharing, we will remember His benefits and rejoice in one another's salvation and renewal. You need to share—to say out loud—how you have depended on God, His Word, and His faithfulness. This empowers others to bear witness to His great name.

Each of us needs to be in fellowship with other believers. Not because it's necessary for salvation, but because it is how we are strengthened. If the reason hasn't sunk in yet, think about how blessings do not flow in only one direction. In fact, I think they are at least tri-directional. We bless the Lord with our heart, soul, and life (that's one); we receive blessing in His benefits (that's a second direction); and when we remember His benefits together in community, it blesses others (that's the third). And that again blesses God, right? So it is a continuous blessing cycle.

Do you remember a time when you shared with another what God had done in your life and the person expressed a growing faith? All of a sudden your hope was their hope. The words from your mouth started to kindle the fire within them. It blessed you because you were empowered to say: "This is who I am, this is what I believe, this is where I stand, and this is where my trust is placed."

And then that blessing cycle continued. I find it so amazing that while we are sharing our faith, blessing Him, and blessing each other, Scripture says He's listening and He hears.

> Then those who feared the LORD spoke to one another,
> And the LORD listened and heard them;
> So a book of remembrance was written before Him
> For those who fear the LORD
> And who meditate on His name.
> (Malachi 3:16 NKJV)

Isn't that priceless? He's hearing you and He's taking notes. He remembers when we remember His benefits. It is your fear (awesome reverence) of the Lord and your faithful pursuit of Him and sharing of Him that causes God to lean in and listen.

I think about the faithful people we can study in the Bible and how so many of them never saw the promises fulfilled. They did not have full revelation of the cross, or the blood, or heaven, yet they walked by faith on what they were given. "Without faith it is impossible to please Him, for he who comes to God must believe that He is, and that He is a rewarder of those who diligently seek Him" (Hebrews 11:6 NKJV).

Do you live, walk, and seek Him with the kind of faith that is based on what you are given? Or do you strive to know how things will turn out and risk uncertainty becoming a divide between you and God's presence? Will you be one who diligently seeks to know Him?

God invites you just as you are,
right here and now,
to know and trust Him.

Join me as we learn to walk with that kind of faith—one that holds strong even when we don't know what is to come. In times of uncertainty, there *is* absolute certainty when you call on God as Creator (*Elohim*), Provider (*Jehovah Jireh*), Healer (*Jehovah Rophe*), Peace (*Jehovah Shalom*), Shepherd (*Jehovah Roi*), and more. When I taught classes on this, I confessed openly that I didn't know how to properly pronounce all the Hebrew names. Chances are they come out of my mouth slightly altered by a Southern twang. But I'm pretty sure that God does not mind our accents or pronunciation blunders. In fact, He probably listens keenly to each of our personal ways of speaking His names and receives joy in our unique inflections and interpretations.

You cannot trust a stranger, and our God has offered us the privilege of knowing Him intimately and personally. We learn to trust Him when we grow in revelation knowledge and understanding of His great name. God invites you just as you are, right here and now, to know and trust Him. Will you accept the invitation and join me on this great adventure of drawing closer to the heart of God?

1

Know Your Purpose in *Elohim*

God Is Your Creator

A sweet and substantial relationship develops between a woman and God when she calls on Him as Creator, All-Sufficient One, Shepherd, Healer, and the other names we will embrace during our time together. Before I did this study, I may have wondered, *What's in a name? Why is it important to know the multiple names of someone?* But even then, had I thought much about it, I would've realized how greatly that knowledge strengthens a relationship. Have you discovered that the better you know a person, the more their name means to you? When you hear it or speak it, that name brings to mind an image and an emotion. The name begins to represent the character and heart of a particular person, not merely a label.

I recall reading and dwelling on Song of Solomon 1:3 (NKJV), "Your name is ointment poured forth," and my heart cried, *Yes it is! Lord, I want to know You more intimately and personally. I want to learn to call on You in a deeper way. A way that will reflect Your character and not merely a label for who You are.* That verse sparked an awareness of how much more I had to grow in my knowledge of my God. I sensed Him responding, "Know Me through My names!"

Perhaps this verse caught my attention because of the personal pain I was feeling deep within my own heart. The image of ointment being gently and tenderly applied to a wound gave me comfort and healing I desperately needed. The words from Song of Solomon, written thousands of years ago, spoke clarity into my haze of sadness and sorrow and beckoned me to come closer and receive the power in the names of God revealed in Scripture.

Sometimes we forget that God is not playing hide and seek with our faith. He is not trying to taunt or frustrate us in our pursuit of Him. It is His heart's desire for us to know the many aspects of His character and to learn to find strength, refuge, and identity in Him through those names. His many names unfold into the deeper heart of His divine nature. Throughout Scripture His many names are used to highlight the unique attributes of His character. With each new level of discovery, we are enriched in faith as we learn to address God with the name that is specific to a particular need we have or blessing we long for.

God's deepest desire is for us to truly know Him. He is not satisfied for us to simply know *about* Him. He wants us to know the genuine depth of His love and provision for us through deep personal revelations of His character. Those personal insights and unveilings are found in His many names. He created us in His image so that we would live in relationship with Him and cleave to Him with deep dependence and unwavering trust. So what better name to start with than the very first name God shared in Scripture and the one that means "creator": *Elohim.*

God often draws us to Himself as our Creator. We are made in the image of God.

> Then God said, "Let Us make man in Our image, according to Our likeness; and let them rule over the fish of the sea and over the birds of the sky and over the cattle and over all the earth, and over every creeping thing that

creeps on the earth." God created man in His own image,
in the image of God He created him; male and female
He created them. (Genesis 1:26-27)

Allow this truth to sink into your inner being for a minute. He prepared His creation with infinite wisdom, perfect order, and meticulous attention to every detail. At the completion of each day's creation, He declared, "It is good." Then He made male and female and gave them rule over all that had been created, and "God saw all that He had made, and behold, it was very good" (Genesis 1:31).

We have been designed with a God-given purpose from the very beginning. No matter what your personal circumstances are, you are not an accident, a mistake, or assigned to a life of pointless, purposeless existence. God's plans and preparations since the beginning of time include you! The prophet Jeremiah spoke these words of promise from God: " 'For I know the plans that I have for you,' declares the LORD, 'plans for welfare and not for calamity to give you a future and a hope' " (Jeremiah 29:11). The message of these words is given in countless ways throughout Scripture to communicate encouragement and a deep sense of purpose. Certainly this insight helps us build our trust in God.

Everything You Need from the Beginning

If we examine the name *Elohim*, a more complete image of God unfolds. *Elohim* is the plural form of the word *"El,"* which means "Strong One." It refers to God, and the plural form of *Elohim* intimates the Trinity. As we spend time in Genesis, we realize that *Elohim* refers to more than one. Genesis 1:26 presents a plural pronoun: "Then God said, 'Let Us make man in Our image, according to Our likeness.' " We can interpret this plural name for God and the interchange of singular and plural pronouns for God in Genesis to represent the Trinity. This idea left me awestruck. At the very beginning of all creation, the fellowship of the Trinity existed in unbroken relationship. Take this incredible truth further: God the Father, God the Son, and God the Holy Spirit together created the world and created you and me. They created us to reflect their very nature and gave us the capacity for deep intimate relationship with the Godhead working in our lives.

An understanding of the power of each part of the Trinity will enable us to find the wholeness we all long for in our relationship with God. Jesus, the Son, is the second person of the Trinity, and He was present at our creation. Colossians 1:16 says, "By Him all things were created that are in heaven and that are on earth" (NKJV). Our way of salvation and our bridge to God was there in the very beginning. The plan of salvation, the cross of Christ, was not an afterthought or a plan B to deal with sin. The perfect, sinless Son of God was present at creation. God the Father, foreseeing the sin of Adam, provided "the Lamb of God who takes away the sin of the world" (John 1:29 NKJV).

> But now, thus says the LORD, your Creator, O Jacob,
> And He who formed you, O Israel,
> "Do not fear, for I have redeemed you;
> I have called you by name; you are Mine!
> When you pass through the waters, I will be with you;
> And through the rivers, they will not overflow you.
> When you walk through the fire, you will not be
> scorched,
> Nor will the flame burn you." (Isaiah 43:1-2)

Redemption is one of those beautiful benefits of His holy name that we are called to remember. Redemption is the gracious gift of God provided through His Son. He has offered to redeem us. He calls us by name. He says, "You are Mine!" *Elohim* declares you are His precious creation.

The sweet gift of being called by God was made very real to me by Margaret, a friend of mine. She has been my prayer partner for many years, and as the day of my daughter Caroline's wedding drew near, Margaret called to say she would like to get together with us to pray for the bride. Years of common sharing and caring have gone into this relationship, and it was with eager expectation that we gathered on the front steps of the wedding site to lift our hearts to God. Margaret prayed something precious and profound. She said, "I don't know why your parents named you Caroline, but God named you before the beginning of time. They chose a name, but God appointed it. Your name means 'strength,' and we see how God ordained strength to mark your character from the time you were a very small child." God named my daughter and let me think I had picked it out! He perfectly named her because He has redeemed her and she belongs to Him. Margaret's prayer was a beautiful reminder and a great faith builder. He is very personally invested in His creation, and we can trust Him. What a sweet picture of our Creator's delight in redeeming and calling us each one by name. He is telling us of His great love and attachment to us. Why would we doubt or resist His plans and purposes for our lives when He exhibits such devotion to His creation?

The most beautiful illustration of His love is when He allows us to become a new creation in Christ (2 Corinthians 5:17) by calling on His name for salvation. *Elohim* called light out of the darkness. He is the same God who creates supernatural light in the soul of man and delivers us from the kingdom of darkness to His marvelous light. Jesus the Son said, "I am the light of the world. He who follows Me shall not walk in darkness, but have the light of life" (John 8:12 NKJV). Being named by God, being called by name, and sharing in His great name are tremendous privileges and responsibilities. I pray that you are filled with a greater understanding of your individual significance to your Creator and that your heart is lifted and encouraged by the Son's gift of redemption for you.

The third person of the Trinity present at creation was the Holy

Spirit. "The Spirit of God was moving over the surface of the waters" (Genesis 1:2). The Holy Spirit does the work of wooing and drawing us to our Creator. When a person looks to the cross of Christ for salvation, the Holy Spirit comes to indwell the believer and hovers over their heart to give assurance and security of eternal salvation. Paul said, "You were sealed with the Holy Spirit of promise, who is the guarantee of our inheritance until the redemption of the purchased possession, to the praise of His glory" (Ephesians 1:14 NKJV). The Holy Spirit is the inner witness of *Elohim* reminding us that we belong to Him and nothing will ever snatch us away.

When I let go of religion and received Jesus as my Redeemer in personal relationship, I was immediately aware of a deep sense of assurance. I had tried to figure out how to know God for many years and took the usual avenues of being good enough or trying harder. But no matter how "on" or "off" I was, I never felt certain I was acceptable. The relief and the freedom from self-effort was an amazing change. It has been more than thirty years since I trusted the blood of Christ to cover my sins. I have floundered and faltered many times. There have been seasons when I have stumbled and fallen along the path. But I have never, ever doubted the presence of the Holy Spirit lifting me up and setting my feet back on the solid rock. The Spirit hovers over His children to guide them all the way through life and into His presence.

We were designed to have abundant life! That is a reality far too few of us are living out. *Elohim* desires His creation to have the Father, Son, and Holy Spirit in fellowship together making our lives complete in Him. If any part of the Trinity is left out of our relationship, we are spiritually incomplete. Let me share a little more what I mean. Acknowledging we believe in God is the first step, but it cannot stop there. Many religions believe

> All you would ever need was present in the moment of your creation.

in a Supreme Being or higher power. But there is much more to our *Elohim*. Look at the profound words written by the apostle John: "In the beginning was the Word, and the Word was with God, and the Word was God. He was with God in the beginning. Through him all things were made; without him nothing was made that has been made. In him was life, and that life was the light of all mankind" (John 1:1-4 NIV). Jesus is our source of eternal life. By believing in Him, we are promised that a river of living water will flow within us. This is the promise of the Holy Spirit, whom all who believe were to receive after Jesus ascended into heaven. He sent His Spirit to empower His children to walk in the truth and the light of His life. *Elohim* has given us His full supply to enable us to reflect His glory.

Before we go any further, will you do a heart check and ask yourself if your life is reflecting a complete image of the Creator?

Have I been reconciled to God through His Son, Jesus? He said, "I am the way, the truth, and the life. No one comes to the Father except through Me" (John 14:6 NKJV). How do you know if the Holy Spirit is at work in your life? Listen to His job description according to Jesus, and you will know: "When he, the Spirit of truth, comes, he will guide you into all the truth. He will not speak on his own; he will speak only what he hears, and he will tell you what is yet to come. He will glorify me because it is from me that he will receive what he will make known to you" (John 16:13-14 NIV).

Before our innermost being was formed, God's image and plan was for our lives to be filled with the Father, and the Son, and the Holy Spirit. That's huge, my friend. That truth alone should give you significance. That should give you a sense of awe and wonder. That should give you an understanding of how precious and important you are.

Sadly, what I have noticed in my life and from observing others over the years is that we can believe in Jesus with all our heart and we can be headed for heaven, yet we still fumble around in the dark saying we don't know where we're going or what our purpose is. We lose sight of, or maybe we never had sight of, the empowering truth that we are created in the image of the Father, Son, and the Holy Spirit.

So the questions we should ask are: Does my life reflect the complete image of my Creator, or is it still simply reflecting a partial image? Do I call on the full power of the name *Elohim*? Am I trusting all the power of the Godhead, the triune that formed me into being?

Just imagine how incredible our lives would be if we walked through our days buoyed by our identity in the Father, Son, and Holy Spirit rather than brought down by false understanding of our worth and discouraged by the struggle to just get by.

God Calls Your Name

Chances are that believing in God's existence is not your obstacle to embracing His comfort and calling. You look out over creation and you see and cannot deny that truth. You observe nature and people and you watch the seasons evolve, and it's clear that there is a witness across the world to God's existence. But how do you know your purpose? How do you have confidence to stand as a miraculous, formed being and then walk with certainty in the right direction for your life? I believe a lot of people have had times or are in times right now in which they feel as if life is happening at a free-fall pace or that they are in a rat race that has no objective and certainly no joy of the Lord. We get to that place because we don't hear the call on our life. And even if we reach out to God and embrace His holy name, somehow we are unable to hear His response: those empowering moments when He calls our name and places a purpose on our life. We see creation's glory but are unable to hear the Creator's message.

Questions about purpose often arise in a person's life when they are living out the version of life or the success that they believed would fulfill them and yet they are not fulfilled. It was this way for me. I remember very clearly when I first started to ask questions about my purpose. I was about 26 years old, and I was doing the things I had dreamed about, planned for, and worked toward; yet, deep within my innermost being I was unsure of my purpose or what difference my life would make.

Maybe you're beginning to grapple with this inner dialogue: *I've got everything that I've planned for at this point in my life. I go to church. I love God, and I want to live for Him. But I don't know if my life, this life, has purpose. Real purpose.*

I believe we get so used to listening to people and the truth of God *through* people that we actually forget to listen to God. No matter what I communicate to you or others encourage you to believe, it will be your tender understanding and trusting of the Lord and your still times of listening to God that will make the truth real for you and life changing.

For example, we cling to the words of people who say, "God has a purpose for your life. God has a plan." We hold out hope for that very thing. Of course we do—we believe in our Lord. But instead of getting to know God's character and spending time with Him in prayer, we expect to see a big blueprint that says, "You're going to do this, and when you're 32 you're going to do that, and by the time you're 38 this will have happened, and all the while you will know this is God's plan for your life."

But how often does life really unfold like this? How often do you encounter people who say that the existence they live is exactly as they had planned? If you are talking to anyone over 30, chances are you are hearing more about how troubles have happened. Loss has happened. Mistakes and recovery have happened.

Every time I read Scripture and study how God interacts with His people, I perceive God nudging them and basically saying, "You put one foot in front of the next, you live by faith, you learn who I am according to My Word, you listen to My Son, the Word that became flesh and lived among us. You allow My Holy Spirit to enlighten you and to lead you and to teach you and to show you truth. I will begin to show you the plan and the purpose for your life."

Redemption is one of those benefits we are called to remember. God says, "'I have redeemed you; I have called you by name'" (Isaiah 43:1). I love that! We are His. The God of the universe, the God beyond the galaxies, called me by name. He's called you by name. This idea became more intimate to me when I spoke to an expectant mom. As she lovingly patted her stomach, she said, "I've got to tell you, I know what I'm going to name her, and I want you to know her name!" She told me what her name was going to be and she said, "I just love it! I love her! I'm having clothes with monograms made!"

There was no doubt that this child's name was already intertwined with pure love in her mother's heart. Before this child was visible or known to the world, she was named, she was deemed precious, and her parents loved her. This is what God is telling us about His love! "I have redeemed you! I know you by name, and I'm attached to you. I love you so much, I am preparing life for you. If you will lean into Me, I will show you the plans and the purposes that I have for your life!"

God's love is real and powerful. It makes me wonder why we are so reluctant to trust Him. Are you open to knowing your gifting and your calling so you can begin to operate in the full image of the One you were created by and for? If you are, it will require you to journey closer to God with the absolute belief that there is a reason you were made. You have to let go of any belief that tells you otherwise.

Elohim Creates Our Good Works

Elohim created you for a purpose. Throughout this personal faith journey to know God through His names, we will keep coming back to trusting God and trusting this specific truth. After all we have learned concerning His personal attention to and investment in our creation, it makes sense that He has designed us with a plan and purpose. When in doubt, you and I can hold tightly to the revelation of Ephesians 2:10: "We are His workmanship, created in Christ Jesus for good works, which God prepared beforehand so that we would walk in them."

Stop with these four words: "We are His workmanship..." Look around at the beauty of creation. Allow your senses to take in the intricate design of nature, the vastness of the night skies, and the miracle of a newborn baby. Now look into the mirror. As His workmanship, *you* are as intricate in design, as wonderful and miraculous to Him, as any part of His creation. If you are artistic or creative in any way, you know the joy and delight of creating, and that's what you are to God. This truth should begin to help us see ourselves and see each other through His eyes instead of our own. Once we are re-created in Christ, our purpose is to be used to accomplish the works He has prepared for us. *Elohim* is waiting to use you. You have an assignment, and He wants you to know it, be equipped for it, and allow Him to use you to accomplish it for His glory. It's all about Him: His workmanship, His good works, and His preplanned purpose for you.

We get anxious about His good works, and we want to figure out which works are appointed for us. Because they are His works, they are revealed to us as we surrender our lives to Him and learn to walk with Him in trust and obedience. We are being trained and equipped every single day. We are reminded by Paul, "Whatever you do in word or deed, do all in the name of the Lord Jesus" (Colossians 3:17 NKJV). Today, whatever God sets before you, it is an opportunity to do it to please Him. It is easy to lose sight of Him when your day is largely comprised of seemingly small and mundane tasks: folding clothes, driving endless carpools, and caring for little messy, whiney people or old, cranky ones. But whatever God puts before you today is an opportunity to be faithful with small things. Let me share a couple of examples of God's workmanship doing His work in ways that point others to Him.

Pastor Eric's heart is burdened for Muslim people in the United States. He is called to minister in one of the darkest, most difficult sections of a large city. He leaves a thriving ministry in a comfortable community and embarks on building one-on-one relationships at a slow and intentional pace in a new area. Every day he humbles himself and allows God to use him to shine the light of Jesus and extend love toward his neighbors and acquaintances. It isn't big or grand. There is no welcoming church office or holy huddle of fellowship. But there is the deep sense of purpose, of being used to accomplish God's appointed work through him.

This spiritual pull toward those in need reminds me of my son, James. His heart was huge, and his love for the people in Africa was deep. He was called to them, lived with them, encouraged and loved them one person at a time. He built genuine relationships, witnessed for Christ, gave whatever he had, and didn't care if anyone ever knew what he was doing. It was a joy to James to be used as His workmanship and to accomplish His good works. We reap benefits when we walk in the purpose God ordains for us, but the greatest benefit is that we bring glory to God and bless His name, "for it is God who works in you to will and to act in order to fulfill his good purpose" (Philippians 2:13 NIV).

He creates His good works in us to fulfill His good purpose. Amen.

Living as a New Creation

Paul is one of our greatest examples of a man who lived his life as a new creation and who knew and professed that the results of his labor had nothing to do with his ability and everything to do with God's ability. Consider his testimony from 1 Corinthians: "By the grace of God I am what I am, and His grace toward me did not prove vain; but I labored even more than all of them, yet not I, but the grace of God with me" (15:10). The grace of God was the reason he was living a radically changed life.

I can hear Paul praising *Elohim*: "My Creator re-created me. I had an image of myself. I was religious, I was important, I was educated, and I had heritage and culture and family connections. I was known, I had influence, I had everything the world says I should in order to have purpose. Then He called me by name. He blinded me with His light on the road to Damascus, and I was transformed. It's only by God's grace that I am what I am. I'm a believer in the risen Lord Jesus; I'm a changed man who lives in the full image of God. His grace toward me was not in vain, not without effect."

Paul's conviction and transformation of heart brings God glory. Great glory. The same is meant to be true in our lives. How tragic it would be if the grace of God poured out for us on Calvary were in vain. God works in our lives the same way He worked in Paul's. Let's look at the steps taken to lead us in our own journey to trust our Creator. Read the miraculous encounter Paul had with Jesus in Acts 9. In those verses, he was called by his Hebrew name, Saul. It was only after the Damascus road encounter that Saul chose to be called Paul, his Roman name. He wanted to be able to reach people for God without his old name and former ways interfering.

He submitted. Saul bowed his knee, head, and heart to give himself over to *Elohim*. In awe of the light and magnificence of Christ, Paul surrendered to God's mercy and forgiveness. In that moment, he became a vessel for God's good works and good pleasure.

He repented. Saul was a helpless man when God spoke to him by name out of heaven and asked him, "Saul, Saul, why are you persecuting Me?" He calls us by name, and He knows what we are doing. The veil of unbelief was lifted, and Saul was able to recognize how far he was from God's purpose. When we fully realize the depth of our sin and the overflowing capacity of His forgiveness, we deeply desire to become the new creation God made us to be.

He surrendered. Once transformed, Saul released self-importance and his personal plans for his life. He became God's workmanship, available to be used by Him, for Him, for His glory. Look at God's appointing words: "He is a chosen instrument of Mine, to bear my name before the Gentiles and kings and the sons of Israel…" (Acts 9:15). God chose a murdering, hate-filled fanatic to carry the gospel all over the then-known world. Saul, filled with the Spirit of God, was enabled to live in the fullness of God.

Freedom from Striving

Our transformation in Christ brings an amazing freedom that covers our lives. Even burdens become blessings when we trust God's intended purpose for us. The places He chooses to use us and give us ministry are often unlikely and unusual. Pastor Eric's burden for Muslims, James's heart for Africans, and a strict Jew (Paul) called to Gentiles are all examples of God's transforming power. I was thinking about our relationship to *Elohim*, and a simple illustration came to my mind. The manufacturer of a product does not ask that product to do something it can't do. For example, Whirlpool would never ask a dishwasher to be a refrigerator. Ford would never ask a car to be a lawnmower. Yet consider how often we challenge our Potter and play out the scene presented in Isaiah 45:9: "Woe to him who strives with his Maker! … Shall the clay say to him who forms it, 'What are you making?'" (NKJV). Here is the root of our strife with our Maker.

Why in the world would we think that the Creator—who made us in His image, who knew us when we were yet unformed—would ask us to do or to be or be a part of anything that we are unsuited, ill-equipped, or unable to do? The key is to yield to His creative hand in your life. It is impossible until we see ourselves as the transformed re-creation of God.

We are His workmanship, not produced generically on an assembly line, but shaped to be unique and blessed by His hands! You are an intricate, one-of-a-kind, valuable, priceless possession of the Maker. You and I may have been living a long time with our own picture of who we are. And frankly, isn't that image hard to uphold and preserve? In fact, it is so hard that we keep trying to re-create who we are rather than spending time with *Elohim* asking Him who we were created to be. Avoiding His truth and refusing to trust *Elohim* leads to so much wasted effort invested in false living.

We are immersed in a cultural mindset that compels us to think, *I'm just going to reinvent myself. I'm going to spend a lot of energy trying to get rid of who I was and become someone new.* Meanwhile, God, *Elohim*, has much more for us. We are trading freedom in Christ for a false, empty version of who we were formed to become. Striving is holding on to that notion that you know what you need for your life. Oh, that's when the starter gun goes off and the tug-of-war between you and the Holy Spirit ensues. You're determined. *I'm going to do this. I'm going to set this up. It's all going to work out my way.* (And by the way, please know that when I say "you," I also mean "me"!) Then we expect the Lord to bless us and our plans. But we are working against God's purpose. Even when we do good things and map out a plan that serves great causes, if we are not doing God's work God's way, then we are striving with our Maker.

The Word has a warning for us about striving with our Maker, about turning around to the Potter and saying, "What are You doing with me? Why are You asking me to do this and that?" What is interesting about this dynamic is that we do this out of an overly developed sense of value or ego *and* also out of a sense of not being worthy of a specific plan from God for our lives. So no matter which side of that spectrum we act from—pride or insecurity—the result is the same: we are creating tension between our spirit and the Holy

Spirit, and we are striving against *Elohim*'s good pleasure in and through us. How exhausting!

His good pleasure is not an activity and it's not a project. It's hard to get that out of our little worker-bee, do-good heads. His good pleasure is for me to live in the fullness of His image. When I do, the good works will constantly reflect back to my Creator.

Many of us as need to hear that and apply it to how we interact with a child, spouse, friend, or someone in our family or faith community. We absolutely must view each child of God as fearfully and wonderfully made. Every person is His workmanship; they are not our workmanship. For a mom this is an especially difficult truth to embrace. It is not our responsibility to craft our children into who we want them to become. Ouch. Take it from someone who has walked long enough raising children and lost one of them…oh, how I beg you, trust that precious created image to the One who made him or her completely and wholly, because He wants to fulfill His purposes in him or her. By letting go of the role of creator, you are surrendering to *Elohim*'s purpose for your life as well.

Trusting God to be in charge of our hearts, minds, spirits, and lives will only happen if we understand purpose in a spiritual sense. Contrary to the meaning of that word in our work and life circles, purpose is not what you do after you put this book down. Purpose is not what you plot out and then carry out. Your purpose is not an action. Your purpose is what you are. Purpose is Whose you are.

I know. This is not the purpose the world teaches. Most living, breathing, working humans equate purpose with career, success, and deliberate action steps toward a goal. It takes time in the Word for this God perspective to sink in, but when it does, you will find freedom in God's purpose for you. When you are striving and plotting and putting energy toward success and quantifiable measures of self-worth, you have veered away from purpose as God intends. And chances are that you are exhausted and ready for an authentic way of being you.

With this perspective, we can sing out to *Elohim* with praise and honor for *who* we are in Him. Our hearts are full because His image lives in us. He glorifies Himself when we are shining as the work of His hands and we say, "Awesome are Your works through the greatness of Your power. It's nothing I do. It's nothing I've set out to accomplish; it's nothing that I am. It's God. It's His awesome power at work in me."

> Shout joyfully to God, all the earth;
> Sing the glory of His name;
> Make His praise glorious.
>
> Say to God, "How awesome are Your works!
> Because of the greatness of Your power Your enemies
> will give feigned obedience to You.
> "All the earth will worship You,
> And will sing praises to You;
> They will sing praises to Your name."
>
> Come and see the works of God,
> Who is awesome in His deeds toward the sons of men.
> (Psalm 66:1-5)

The world says, "Wait and see. Show me the evidence and then I will come." But I love this passage of Scripture because it claims, "Come and see." This is how we praise God and invite others to trust His holy name. We call others to come and see, to get into His Word. Come and allow Him to be a part of your life and trust Him to speak personally to you. Come and see what it is to live by faith. The believer, the person living in the image of God, says, "Come, and you will see. I'm certain of it. *Elohim*, who created you, will never disappoint you. Oh, how *Elohim* does not disappoint!"

Encountering Elohim

Trusting Elohim

1. Trust in your identity as God's wonderful creation: "I will praise You, for I am fearfully and wonderfully made; marvelous are Your works, and that my soul knows very well" (Psalm 139:14 NKJV). How does believing that purpose is who you are, and not what you do, radically change your mindset, your burden to succeed, or your worries that you aren't good enough?

2. Ask the Holy Spirit of the living God to come in and fill you with streams of living water so that you might live in the purpose that God has placed before you today, which is simply to bring Him pleasure and to give glory to His name so that the world will have accurate estimation of who God is.

Remembering the Benefits of Elohim

1. The Creator calls you by name. You were formed by His hands. Walk in this confidence. See how it deepens your connection to His heart when you pray. Experience the reassurance of your identity as God's child. When you feel alone or lost, hold tightly to this truth.

2. The Trinity was with you from the very beginning. And the Father, Son, and Holy Spirit are with you as you are shaped into a new creation. Trust this power in your life. Consider which difficulty you are struggling with or striving against. Submit this struggle to *Elohim* today, right now. Let Him make something holy and new from your offering.

Blessing Elohim

1. Bless *Elohim* by showing your trust in Him. Make it apparent to those around you that you place your faith only in Him. When the fruit of your life is evidence of that trust, you bring glory to *Elohim*. Let your actions and words say "Come and see" to those in your life. What purpose is God calling you to that will lead others to praise Him? Walk in this with confidence.

2. Do as Paul did: submit, repent, and surrender. Consider making a commitment to walk through these three steps in one specific area of your life. This action blesses your Creator and leads to transformation. Pay attention to how your life changes in this area.

Praying to Elohim

Elohim, *I praise Your name for creating me and all the wonders of the earth and sky. As I begin this journey of drawing close to You and calling out Your holy name, Lord, show me what it is that has prevented me from trusting You completely in the past. I want to let go of any doubt and sense of unworthiness so that I walk boldly and humbly on the path You formed from the beginning. I step with awe into my life today because I claim the truth that You—the Father, Son, and Holy Spirit—created me in Your image.*

I feel lighter and more at peace as I release my desire to strive against You, Elohim. *Show me how to trust You and the journey ahead so that the fruit of my life becomes the good works and good purposes of Your hand. I praise and worship You,* Elohim, *our Creator, in Jesus' name. Amen.*

2

Become Satisfied and Able Through *El Shaddai*

God Is Your All-Sufficient One

Everyone wants satisfaction. You may remember the lyrics to a rock song made popular by Mick Jagger and the Rolling Stones. It was titled, "(I Can't Get No) Satisfaction." It reached the top of the charts at the time of its release in 1965. It voices the sentiments of thousands and thousands of people in desperate search of satisfaction in life. The yearning for satisfaction seems to be hardwired in the human heart. It compels us to constantly search and strive for more. The real problem seems to be discerning, "More of what?" Until we can identify the genuine root of our yearning, we are driven by restless wanderlust. The inner being struggles and strives because of spiritual alienation from God our Creator.

The search usually launches us down various avenues offered by the world as possible solutions for our gnawing hunger for satisfaction: relationships, all sorts of physical desires and activities, intellectual pursuits and accomplishments, personal and professional status, and achievements, to name a few. But the genuine source for our soul satisfaction is found in relationship with *El Shaddai*. He is the God of all power who nourishes, supplies, and satisfies. In Him the restless, wandering, discontent soul can find all that is needed to fulfill the longing deep within every human heart.

As we discovered in the last chapter, *El* means God. And the Hebrew root word of *Shaddai* is *Shad*, which means "breast," "nourish," "supplies," and "satisfies." *El Shaddai* feeds, supplies, nourishes, and satisfies His children. As I visited the meanings of this name of God, I had the picture in my mind of a nursing baby. That image alone made me feel tender and grateful toward our loving God. If you've ever had a nursing baby, or if you've ever been left to take care of a nursing baby, you know from experience that there is absolutely nothing else that will satisfy that nursing baby but Mama. When a baby is hungry, she leans in to her mother, roots into her natural source of nourishment. A mother or caregiver will hold the baby close to satisfy and nourish. A pacifier or a finger placed in the baby's little mouth might soothe him for a brief while, and water from a bottle will temporarily fill his belly; but eventually, the child needs something beyond substitutions for nourishment.

David, the psalm writer, wrote it this way: "For He has satisfied the thirsty soul, and the hungry soul He has filled with what is good" (Psalm 107:9). Nothing will satisfy our soul except that which comes from God. If we don't know God as *El Shaddai*, or we forget that He is the all-sufficient source of our strength and blessings, we turn to substitutions for satisfaction and we try to take care of things in our own power. The Bible has many examples of restless wanderers who needed to be rerouted because they were going to the wrong places and people and priorities to find soul satisfaction. Scripture reveals how God responds to His children and redirects them to His sufficiency.

Abram, before he was Abraham, is one of the examples we can turn to. He was deep in discontentment when God presented Himself as *El Shaddai*. But before we look at Abram's encounter with *El Shaddai*, let's look at what caused his shift from hopeful to impatient, from trusting to doubting. As we explore what happened to turn Abram into a child who looked for satisfaction apart from his

God, we will surprisingly see ourselves. Or at least I see myself at every turn in this story! And we will discover how to lean in to and lean on *El Shaddai*. My prayer is that you and I will say and believe about our God, as David did, "You open Your hand and satisfy the desire of every living thing" (Psalm 145:16 NKJV).

Trusting God's Promises

Abram had been walking with God. He was not footloose and reckless. From Genesis 12 we can understand that God had already told Abram that He was going to make him a father of many nations. He gave him a personal promise. God gave him just enough to go on. And to paraphrase the first three verses, He basically told Abram, "I want you to go from your father's house to a land that I will show you. I will make you a great nation, and I will bless you and I will make your name great. You will be a blessing. I will bless those who bless you, and I will curse those who curse you."

Abram responded to God with obedient faith. He went forward in the direction of those promises. He and his family went to Canaan. But oh, there were detours. And oh, did they ever have some drama. And oh, were mistakes made along that path. And all the while, Abram and his wife, Sarai (before God changed her name to Sarah), believed they would conceive so that they would see God's promise of many descendants become a reality.

They waited. They waited. And then they waited some more.

Years later they still did not have offspring. The baby representing the fulfillment of God's promises, the hope of nations, and the beginning of generations of descendants had not been conceived. Empty arms, an empty cradle, and empty dreams caused them to wonder if what they'd heard had been empty promises from God.

This messed with Abram's faith. You know he was imagining himself as a happy daddy; there were going to be children running all around the yard by then. Abram was in this vast, empty waiting room of faith. However, instead of holding tight to his belief in God's sufficiency and faithfulness, he resorted to trying to help God.

He made decisions that came from doubting God's promise—actually, from a lack of trust in God, period.

So, like maybe we have done a time or two, Abram chose to listen to a voice other than God's voice. He put his faith in the voice and the words of Sarai, who encouraged him to have a child with her handmaid, Hagar. Everything changed when he let go of God's word while he was waiting. Instead, he chose to believe that it was up to *him* to take matters into his own hands and push his way out of the waiting room. His determination to self-satisfy his desire for God's promises to come to fruition caused him to forever change the course of his life and history. What a mess he made!

I think it is common for people to seek meaning or identity in relationships, hobbies, activities, work, achievements, or material comforts and securities. Can you remember a time when you tried to satisfy yourself or push through an agenda in your own power? Like a pacifier, perhaps something satisfied you for a period of time; maybe, like water from a bottle, it filled you up long enough that you thought you had found *the* thing to gratify you and please you. That is until reality set in and you were left depleted and with an awareness that your inability to wait for God's sufficiency caused you, like Abram, to mess things up.

When you are waiting on God,
God is working in your life.

Weary in the Waiting Room

I have been in God's waiting room during my life. It is a place where many of us become so frustrated that we are tempted toward disbelief because the waiting is discouraging. Nobody wants to be disappointed, especially by God, so it seems easier or safer to let go of that original nudge and belief, doesn't it?

There was a time when God clearly gave me a promise that was personal and specific in relation to a situation and a person. He confirmed the belief through the years, but there was no sign of the promise being fulfilled. Time and time again I thought, *Lord, how long will this take?* I kept a record of every year that the promise remained outstanding, unfulfilled. In fact, I dated it in my Bible. Maybe I wanted to be sure God was reminded too! With each passing year, I grew more nervous. I felt fear rise up, which made me question whether I had dreamed it. When this inkling of doubt surfaced, I went to the Word of God for reassurance. I would recommit to hold on to God's faithful character. I would refuse to let the lack of tangible evidence undermine my faith in God's word.

Maybe today you are in this place that feels like a waiting room where you keep watch for something that looks like God's promise. Too much time has passed, and the reason you're waiting has become less clear and more removed from your priorities. Have you lost focus and hope?

If we respond as Abram did, we wear down. We break down. Maybe you've been waiting for wellness, for a spouse, for a baby, or for somebody you love to get saved. Maybe you're waiting for a job or a move. You're waiting to feel accepted or to experience a milestone. How are you waiting? Have you come to a place where you're starting to doubt? *Did I hear that? Did He call me here? Is this what He meant; is this what He's going to do?*

When you are waiting on God, God is working in your life. *El Shaddai* is all-mighty, or all-powerful. His perfect nature tenderly provides and sustains while you wait with Him. His *sufficiency* gives us the strength and patience to endure the waiting. Like I said, He supplies every single thing for His children.

God Works Even Through Our Blunders

By the time Abram had his encounter with *El Shaddai*, he had tried to "fix" the situation rather than wait on his all-sufficient God. Even by having a son with Hagar, Abram still doubted God's promise was possible. The possibility of the original plan unfolding seemed more ludicrous than ever. After all, at that point Abram was 99 years old and Sarai was 89 years old. But Abram was about to experience the reality: with God all things are possible.

> Now when Abram was ninety-nine years old, the Lord appeared to Abram and said to him,
>
> "I am God Almighty;
> Walk before Me, and be blameless.
> I will establish My covenant between Me and you,
> And I will multiply you exceedingly."
>
> Abram fell on his face, and God talked with him, saying,
>
> "As for Me, behold, My covenant is with you,
> And you will be the father of a multitude of nations.
> No longer shall your name be called Abram,
> But your name shall be Abraham;
> For I have made you the father of a multitude of
> nations." (Genesis 17:1-5)

Do you see how God reinforced that He was going to do it all? He showed up in Abram's life and declared that He would do these things in and through Abram. The same is true for you and me. *El Shaddai* comes to each of us and declares that He will do it. He's telling us that we don't have to. In fact, we can't do what needs to be done, but God can and will. Do we believe Him? Do we answer the call to walk with God and be blameless and wholehearted? Or are we tempted to revert to old ways, to old measures of safety that the world offers, just because we are tired of waiting on God's best?

In the waiting room, can you ignore the messages, distractions, disruptions, anxieties, and temptation to entertain substitutions for God's sufficiency? Can you put to rest the frustrations that seem to claim no one is ever going to call your name? I want to encourage you to go back to God's Word and His promise to you. I can assure you that your circumstance will not look the way you thought it would look, and I can tell you that when God does nudge you further, it won't necessarily be in the timing you wanted or imagined. Are you like me? When you prayed and received hope from God, you were certain that the unfolding of His purpose in you was going to look a certain way. But God's word to you will not fail.

Our hope for our circumstance rises when we see God's interaction with Abram in Genesis 17. It had been 13 years since God had made His initial promise to Abram, and Abram's household was erupting with chaos. One man, two women, and one baby. It was not what God wanted for them. Yet God appeared.

God shows up in the chaos. And He shows up as *El Shaddai*. This should be a great source of encouragement! If your life is in turmoil because of the choices you have made and the voices you have listened to, remember that your almighty, sustaining, and supplying God will show up and speak words of truth and direction into your life. Listen carefully.

It's as if He said to Abram: "You've taken your eyes off of Me; you're looking at the circumstances. You're looking at your old body and her old body. All you can see is two old people, so you determined that you would have to work this promise of Mine out." God's comments could have ended there. He could've pointed out the mess Abram and Sarai had made and then left them to deal with it. He could've revoked His covenant. But instead He *renewed* His covenant with this blessed couple by giving them new names.

Abraham means "father of many nations." How could Abraham doubt in the spiritual waiting room ever again when his own name was his reminder of God's faithfulness and power and of *El Shaddai's* sufficiency in all things? God also changed Sarai's name to *Sarah*, which means "mother of nations." In that act, God made it so that when Abraham and Sarah heard their names, they would be reminded of their purpose in His plan. They most definitely would forever remember His benefits, blessings, and promises.

Why? Because *El Shaddai* completes His good work.

I am in awe and filled with gratitude when I witness how *El Shaddai* treats His children after they have muddled and fumbled with His plan. You see, God started a good work in Abraham when He called him out of his home in Haran and into the land of Canaan. Abraham's survival was God's doing, not his. The purpose and vision he was supposed to follow was God's purpose and vision, not his own. Just this morning I read a statement from a young man whom God has called to be a pastor. He said, "This was not the plan I had for my life, that's for sure."

If God has called your name—if He's called you out of darkness into His marvelous light—He has started a good work in you. He started a good work in me, and His Word says He will carry it on to completion. We are not responsible for the good work done through us. As He said to Abraham, "My might is sufficient" for what appears to be a dead, hopeless, misunderstood, impossible dream. Do you have a dead, hopeless, seemingly impossible dream on the radar screen of your life right now? Today you can decide to believe as Abraham learned to believe and as the apostle Paul later proclaimed, "He who has begun a good work in you will complete it until the day of Jesus Christ" (Philippians 1:6 NKJV). When God renamed Abraham, his life purpose became crystal clear, and he focused on God's power, not his own. Look at Paul's declaration concerning Abraham in Romans 4:20-21: "He did not waver in unbelief but grew strong in faith, giving glory to God, and being fully assured that what God had promised, He was able also to perform." The days of leaning on his own understanding were over. From that point forward, Abraham was fully assured that God keeps His word. If God promised, He will perform it. From my own experiences I can testify that what God performs far exceeds my performance! Being fully assured is a beautiful benefit of knowing God as your *El Shaddai*.

Blameless Before God

We encounter God's goodness as He expressed His intention to carry out His good work in Abraham despite his mistakes and unfaithfulness. Instead of spending hours chastising Abraham, God extended instruction and reinforced His covenant: "I am God Almighty; walk before Me, and be blameless. I will establish My covenant between Me and you, and I will multiply you exceedingly" (Genesis 17:1-2).

I wonder how God could or why He *would* show up and ask Abraham to be blameless when he's obviously to blame for the tumultuous situation. *Really, God, how could You believe in Abraham again?*

In this encounter, we learn how *El Shaddai* will hold the standard up for us, give us the instruction, and tell us what we need to do and where we need to go to get our feet back on the right path. He is the God of the second chance and third and fourth, and on and on. This exchange between *El Shaddai* and Abraham also reveals how we might respond to His divine mercy. Thankfully, Abraham, in that moment in *El Shaddai's* presence, really got it. All of it. The mercy, the redemption, and the importance of God's sufficiency. He didn't start making excuses. He didn't point a finger at Sarah or to any one of the obstacles that sparked his dissatisfaction and ill-fated decisions to do things his own way. He didn't start rambling about his woes or his wants. No, he fell on his face. Can you imagine the extent of his gratitude?

The newly named Abraham's response reflected his deeper revelation of the character of his God. He fell on his face, and when he got up he took action in obedience. He took his son, Ishmael, conceived by his own plan rather than God's, and then he took every man in his household, and they were all circumcised in an act of immediate obedience to what God had declared He wanted Abraham to do as a sign of the covenant. God didn't want Abraham to hide or cower; He wanted him to step up and step out, and that's what he did.

> Our all-mighty, all-sufficient God shows up even when we mess up.

Because God is our Redeemer, He's able to take what we mess up and breathe new life into it. When in your life have you messed up out of stubbornness and determination to act in self-sufficiency or out of frustration with your prolonged time in the waiting room? If you'll surrender every part of you back to God and fall on your face, God will show you the way forward. He will bless you. And He will use that detour. He will use the tangled and complicated results of surrendered self-sufficiency. It's not wasted. Your path might look different from God's original plan for you, but it is not a worthless path. Grace makes sure of that. Nothing is wasted when surrendered into God's hands.

If you are worried about your calling or are hearing a word of promise from God and don't feel worthy or adequate, well, that's perfect. The point is that God is worthy and more than adequate. You are the child of *El Shaddai*, and He knows all your warts, all your dark places, all your struggles and secrets. Step out! And walk before

Him with integrity of heart. Why? Because He's got this, whatever "this" is in your life, and He's got you.

Is there an area of your life that God has been asking you to give over to Him in obedience? This might be painful to do at first, but it's a necessary step if you're going to walk blamelessly. Surrender "I try and I try and I try" and say, "*El Shaddai* is my soul's satisfaction!"

God's Exceeding Abundance in Action

I have had an encounter with *El Shaddai* in a very personal way. In fact, the story I am sharing may have truly been my first experience fully understanding and trusting Him as the mighty God who nurtures and supplies. He called me to go on a trip to Kenya. Well, that doesn't seem crazy to ask of someone, does it? But my heart was initially stricken with disbelief and self-doubt. You see, God was calling me to go to where my son, James, had died just ten months before.

He told me to leave the safety of my home and the comfort and protection of my grieving time and go to the land of Kenya—a land that I would forever be tied to through James and also through *El Shaddai*. Make a note that God didn't only call people in the Bible to new lands. He calls you, me, and all His followers to new lands, new vistas, new perspectives, and new hopes all the time.

In my brokenness, I surrendered to *El Shaddai's* request, but believe me, before I gave over to the idea I was pretty sure that this could be a mistake. I was waiting for healing from the grief. I was holing up in self-protection because my wounded heart was so fragile. But beyond me, the circumstances, plans, and arrangements for the itinerary were changed, rearranged, and reworked in such a way that it was clear to me that there was no explanation in my heart for going except God had orchestrated it.

During that time, I would waver whenever I immersed myself in the questions, fears, anxieties, and evidence of my inability. In fact, I doubted God because I was looking at my weakness and not at His strength. *Is this what I really should be doing? Am I ready? Can I do this?* I only had peace when I turned my focus to God's Word and His calling on my heart. I kept my eyes on Him because it was very clear I couldn't do this, but God could.

In His sufficiency, He sent people to me during the 16 weeks of preparation time before we went, and they would have words from God. You see, God doesn't show up in our lives like He did in Abraham's life, but He appears in so many other ways. We have His Word, which is filled with Abraham's example and those of countless others. We have His Holy Spirit living inside of us to guide and teach us. And then we have fellowship with other believers. He showed up in my life through a series of connections with people. I'd even say random people because they weren't people I had previously had regular contact with. But of course, they were not random—they were handpicked by Him to speak truth to me. They'd bring a word to me. They'd say they were praying and that God had given them a particular verse to share to encourage me.

When we arrived in Kenya, my initial list of reasons not to go was still making itself known: I didn't feel ready, I didn't want to do this, it seemed dark and depressing, the task seemed overwhelming, I was weary. Yet, even as those thoughts of inability swirled in my mind, I knew God was calling me to walk before Him, blameless and trusting. I knew that He was reminding me of the promise and the response revealed through Paul:

> "My grace is sufficient for you, for My strength is made perfect in weakness." Therefore most gladly I will rather boast in my infirmities, that the power of Christ may rest upon me. Therefore I take pleasure in infirmities, in reproaches, in needs, in persecutions, in distresses, for

Christ's sake. For when I am weak, then I am strong.
(2 Corinthians 12:9-10 NKJV)

I had a whole lot of infirmities to boast about, let me tell you. So I gave my weaknesses to God, and He gave me His strength. That strength was about to be tested in Maasailand. Let me set the desolate scene. The land does not scream "sufficiency and satisfaction" by a long shot. As far as one can see, there is brown dirt and scrub trees with big, thorny points on them. There are goats, cows, and more dirt. And the animal dung of course. There's nothing green. Every now and then there is a circle of those scrubby plants and inside that area there is a compound with a hut. That's it. And that day we were in one of those spots with a church. It was a shed with a tin roof and a makeshift back on it.

The only things to contrast that brown, hard land were the presence of God and the precious, beautiful people with brilliant red wraps and multicolored beads. As these people gathered, I started rehearsing the reason I was there, hoping to build up my courage: *Okay, awesome, I can do this. We're going to teach on the cross of Christ and that without the cross of Christ, nothing else makes any sense. I did my homework; I am prepared. Teach the cross. Yes.* And then my weaknesses made themselves known. I felt sickened by the magnitude of my ineptitude. My nerves were rattled, and I was sweating profusely. About the time I was supposed to stand up and share, my self-talk had really shifted: *I don't have anything to say. I have no way to relate. There's nothing I can give.*

Shaking, I stood up. I lifted my gaze to look out at the gathering of women. All these beautiful, dark-skinned women who were called mamas. I took in the sight of how many of them had babies tied on their backs and toddlers jumping on their legs or climbing on their laps, crying. Mamas were nursing newborns.

I couldn't hide behind anything because there wasn't a podium. I had a translator, but I wondered what good that would do if I had nothing to offer these mamas. But in that moment when I felt empty of any and every thing, God showed up. I promise you, just like He did to Abraham, He made His presence known to me. He spoke to my heart: "Lean in to Me, nestle right up under My mighty right arm. Latch on, Jan. Latch on. I've got everything you need." I heard and trusted Him. I opened my mouth, and He filled it with His message to His precious people.

El Shaddai showed up in that hot, crowded tin shed. God started to give out His promises to the people there. God was moving in that barren land. And God told those people how much He loved them. His message began to minister and to draw and to woo hearts and to save souls. And God's sufficiency was fully evident.

God showed Himself as *El Shaddai* in a mighty way and that moment, that day, that trip was all to His glory. "Now to Him who is able to do exceedingly abundantly above all that we ask or think, according to the power that works in us, to Him be glory in the church by Christ Jesus to all generations, forever and ever. Amen" (Ephesians 3:20-21 NKJV).

God is able to do exceedingly abundantly above all that we ask or think. He is exceedingly abundantly able to take all the human frailty you surrender to Him and turn it to and for His glory. So, my friend: bring your weakness, bring your infirmity, bring your inadequacy, bring your brokenness, bring your fear, bring your disappointment, bring the changes that life has required and that you resist.

Bring each and every one of these and anything else that represents your inability and powerlessness to the hand of *El Shaddai*, the one who is all-sufficient. And without it being contrived or deliberate, you will discover that you are walking before Him and you are blameless. Therefore, God Almighty is able to supply you with all that you need. That is the power of *El Shaddai*.

Encountering El Shaddai

Trusting El Shaddai

1. Put your faith and trust in *El Shaddai* today. Write down an area of your life in which you long for God's satisfaction and sufficiency. Read and memorize the following verse: "God is able to make all grace abound toward you, that you, always having all sufficiency in all things, may have an abundance for every good work" (2 Corinthians 9:8 NKJV). Stand strong on this promise for your need today.

2. Trust that God wants to reestablish relationship and covenant with you even if you have made a mess. Reflect again on what *El Shaddai* told Abraham: "I am God Almighty; walk before Me, and be blameless. I will establish My covenant between Me and you" (Genesis 17:1-2). What good work, what covenant has God established with you?

Remembering the Benefits of El Shaddai

1. Are you having a spiritual waiting room experience now? In what ways do you seek to take control of the situation from God? Commit to spending more time in His Word so that you are listening to His voice and not to distractions. Make a running list of the promises God fulfills for His children throughout Scripture. You will be encouraged.

2. Your chaos is not too much for *El Shaddai*. Nor are your mistakes and times of stumbling. Identify your brokenness and weaknesses. In fact, you can even celebrate these because they,

more than strengths, will lead you to lean on His sufficiency and eternal ability. He will not fail you.

Blessing El Shaddai

1. When is the last time you fell on your face and gave God your full and undivided attention? Start with a surrendered heart today in His holy presence. That will bless *El Shaddai*, and it will prepare your heart and spirit to hear His leading, promises, and assurances along your journey.

2. Think of my example from Maasailand of God's great sufficiency surpassing my worries and insufficiencies so I could be a conduit of His love to the faithful people who worshipped with gladness. What is your own Maasailand circumstance? Give it to *El Shaddai* so that His sufficiency flows through you and blesses Him and His people. Become a vessel for His message and love today. Remember that you do not do this in your power, but in His.

Praying to El Shaddai

Thank You for showing Yourself to Your children in new ways, El Shaddai. *I fall on my face today in Your grace-filled presence and ask for Your plan for my life. I thank You, Lord, for the desire to be obedient. It is in worshipping You and obeying You that I can walk before You blamelessly and allow You to be* El Shaddai *for all that I need. My circumstances and I are never outside of the reach of Your sufficiency. Today I surrender to You the following needs of my life:*

With gratitude and hope, I ask for You to be made real in my life; lead me to Your presence, El Shaddai. *In Your matchless and mighty name I pray.* Amen.

3

Trust the Unlimited Supply of *Jehovah Jireh*

God Is Your Provider

Do you ever wake up in the morning with a heavy heart? Do you ever have the thought that "this thing," whatever it is that burdens you, will never settle in your spirit? Such things can stay with us for long seasons. You may also have had stretches of peace and rest when this thing was kept at a distance. God, in His goodness and mercy, gives us a break from time to time. Yet, in time, we are likely to admit: "My thoughts, my prayers, and my energy often return to this one thing that God has allowed in my life."

Do you welcome that thing with confidence and assurance in the Lord, or do you look up with a sense of dread and defeat? While some people face job changes or transitions and new beginnings, others face life changes—those brought on by loss, betrayal, or trials. All these circumstances and so many others can trigger within us an initial response of fear rather than faith. When we turn to *Jehovah Jireh*, our Provider, we discover the way to faith in all situations and uncertainties. If we look at the word *provision*, it gives us insight into *Jehovah Jireh*. *Provision* is to see beforehand and provide in advance. God prepares in advance for what we will need during our troubles and beyond. This is our great peace, my friend. With

God, seeing *is* foreseeing. So from the very beginning, God knows the ending. And He prepares and provides for us from beginning to end, including the season when we bear the uncertainty of that thing that weighs on our hearts.

For Abraham, this thing was the promise of a descendant, a son. Remember that Abraham's son, Isaac, had been promised from the beginning of Abraham's walk with God. But this thing did not happen in the timing he and Sarah had hoped for and expected. So they spent many years, many mornings waking to this burden of an unfulfilled promise on their hearts. They spent all that time waiting and wondering and trying to work it out *for* God. They tried hard to fulfill this promise in their own power, and they failed. After all of the years, all of the struggles, and all of the self-effort, that promise finally resulted in faith becoming sight, and that child, named Isaac, became a reality because of God's provision.

We have every indication that Isaac's parents were thrilled to have a child from their marriage. Isaac was growing and thriving. His name means "laughter," so he must have been a happy, fun, enjoyable child to have in the home. And every indication in the Bible during this time is that Isaac was growing up to be an honorable, God-fearing young man. The family was so glad to be together. How they must've delighted in their season of peace and rest. That is, until a new and unthinkable thing appeared in Abraham's life.

God spoke the unimaginable and tested Abraham: "Take now your son, your only son, whom you love, Isaac, and go to the land of Moriah, and offer him there as a burnt offering on one of the mountains of which I will tell you" (Genesis 22:2).

If that isn't a possible faith game changer, then what is?

When God Asks the Impossible

Have you experienced the shockwave of a change that rippled through your life and your heart? Did you get up one day and circumstances were dramatically altered? You were going along just like you'd planned and then, without warning, everything shifted and nothing seemed sure or familiar. That's what it must've felt like for Abraham that day. When he got up, life seemed to be on course according to God's promise. And then God spoke this inconceivable thing into his life.

Even if your thing is quite different, there are three truths we can gain from Abraham's story that can help us understand God and why we are sometimes called to circumstances utterly beyond our human comprehension or strength.

1. Today is preparation for tomorrow. We do not know what God will allow into our lives tomorrow, and today is preparation for what tomorrow may bring.

2. God chooses the thing. Whatever it is, God chose it and allowed it. He wants to use this thing in our lives to draw us to Him and to help us discover who He is. As *Jehovah Jireh*, He provides everything in our life, including ways to use these opportunities to lean into Him. We do not get to choose what He is going to use in our lives. There have been times in my life when I have said, "I do not want to be in this club. This is not where I want to have ministry, Lord." Then He reminds me that He chooses where, when, and how to press me to Himself.

3. God tests His people. This is not an easy truth for everyone to accept, let alone embrace. Isn't this a tough revelation about God? Oftentimes this truth raises the difficult question: "These people love the Lord, follow God, and obey His Word, so why would God allow something like that to happen in their lives?"

Why, Lord? Have you asked this about your circumstance or on behalf of a friend? We can come to this place of questioning in our darkest hour or when the thing that weighs on our hearts awakens us too many mornings in a row. Maybe it has been the question on our lips when we sense God directing us in a way that stuns us and makes us want to run the other direction.

This must be how Abraham felt and thought. Why would God ask him to sacrifice his son? He had obeyed God. He had left his home and done everything God had asked of him along the way. Abraham was not selfish with his nephew Lot; he had given him the better plot of land. Abraham did everything that he could do. Even when he fumbled and tried to do things in his own power (and failed), his heart was always that of a man who wanted to be faithful to God. So why would God show up one morning and ask Abraham to sacrifice Isaac? Because...God tests His people. It is as simple and as difficult as that.

If our circumstance makes us feel like we are being picked on, singled out, or chosen in a way we don't want to be chosen by God, maybe it would help to remember that God even tested Jesus. Jesus! Before Jesus began His public ministry, He "was led up by the Spirit into the wilderness to be tempted by the devil" (Matthew 4:1). God allowed this to happen in Jesus' life. Not only had Jesus been prepared for the endurance of this test, but the test itself prepared Jesus for His ministry and His death, which served to glorify His Father.

God times the testing, He determines what the testing will be, and He determines the level of the test. While we might want to ask, "When Lord? Why Lord?" what we need to ask ourselves is, "If I know that the test is a possibility, will I allow Him to prepare me, equip me, and provide all that I need in order to pass the test in a way that will glorify Him?" Abraham answered yes.

❈❈❈❈❈❈❈❈❈❈❈❈❈❈

Crises do not build character, they reveal character.

Prepared to Receive Provision

On the day the sacrifice was to happen, Abraham surely set out with a heavy heart. I wonder what Abraham was concentrating on when he packed the provisions and told Isaac, "We're going to go on a journey." I wonder what he was thinking when he asked his two servants to go with them and whether his voice shook when he told Sarah, "We're going to be gone for several days." What was he thinking when he and Isaac climbed up Mount Moriah by themselves?

Based on what Scripture tells us about Abraham's reaction and responses, we find that all of his yesterdays devoted to knowing, growing, trusting, and walking with God were equipping him for this time. He must have recalled, "This is what God said. This is what God told me to do. This is where God led me." He must have clung to the word of God in his life. How Abraham had lived his life up until that day had prepared him—even for this.

I believe Abraham chose to remember and recall all of the promises God had given him. I believe he remembered the character of *El Shaddai*, who had already shown Himself to Abraham as the All-Sufficient One. How God had provided for him all his days prepared Abraham—even for this.

His journey and his relationship with God prepared him to concentrate on God every step of the way rather than concentrating on the circumstances of his life. Abraham's trust in God was what allowed him to turn to the servants that went with him and say, "I and the lad will go over there; and we will worship and return to you" (Genesis 22:5). As he spoke this, Abraham might have thought, "I'm not sure how all of this is going to come to pass, but I know God's word is true."

Our Character and His

Crises do not build character, they reveal character. When a crisis comes, you begin to see the true character of a person; the fabric of a person's spirit is revealed. Abraham went forward that difficult day trusting God wholly. He had already established in his heart that God was God and that he would follow Him all of his days. He knew God to be trustworthy and true. He had no reason to doubt God's goodness. Even if Abraham couldn't understand why this was happening, God's trustworthiness was already established in his heart.

Abraham's character was revealed, and he was shown to be obedient, faithful, and trusting of his God. Second Timothy 1:12 says, "I know whom I have believed and am persuaded that He is able to keep what I have committed to Him until that Day" (NKJV). If Abraham had known 2 Timothy, I believe he would have been quoting it all the way up the mountain. He might have thought, *This doesn't make sense. This is not adding up. This is so painful. This is so personal and so costly, but I know whom I have believed.*

Are you persuaded that He is able? Or are you concentrating on how difficult the thing is in your life? It may be your marriage, your finances, your job, your health, or a lack of knowing what you're supposed to be doing and where you're supposed to be going. It could be an interpersonal relationship or a decision you made in the past that continues to come up.

Does this thing in your life reveal a character woven with fear and doubt or threaded with trust and faith? No matter your answer today, in this moment, you can choose to cling to the character of God, the One who is bigger and is able to keep what you have committed to Him.

Surrendering to God's Provision

Hebrews 11:17 says, "By faith Abraham, when he was tested, offered up Isaac" (NKJV). Oh, it was a huge test. It was an advanced placement kind of test. Abraham didn't know the plan, the outcome, or the result of his obedience. Maybe he believed God had the power to bring Isaac back to life. But he didn't know what would happen, and he still went forward with a heart of surrender.

What is God asking you to surrender? A disappointment, a dream, or maybe a broken dream? Maybe this thing appeared to be a gift from God, and now it seems that God is requiring it *from* you. Are you willing to trust God's word and trust God's work even if it costs you something?

Abraham went forward in this unthinkable test even though he knew that the cost would be the sacrifice of the child he held so dear. The story unfolds with the tension and suspense of a spellbinding thriller. So much so that as you read it, you might want to call out to Abraham, "No!" You might find that you can barely handle the thought of this test, even though it isn't the one God has asked of you specifically. Abraham's faithfulness is all the more illuminated because this test breaks our hearts.

> Abraham took the wood of the burnt offering and laid it on Isaac his son, and he took in his hand the fire and the knife. So the two of them walked on together. Isaac spoke to Abraham his father and said, "My father!" And he said, "Here I am, my son." And he said, "Behold, the fire and the wood, but where is the lamb for the burnt offering?" Abraham said, "God will provide for Himself the lamb for the burnt offering, my son." So the two of them walked on together. (Genesis 22:6-8)

Now we start to squirm. Now we might even want to shout to Isaac: "Don't go! Don't follow your father. Don't you see what is about to happen?" But Isaac's trust in his father also became a remarkable side story of faith and devotion. As Isaac followed the leading of his earthly father, Abraham pressed on to follow the lead of his heavenly Father. He prepared the altar and prepared his son to be the sacrifice. "Then they came to the place of which God had told him; and Abraham built the altar there and arranged the wood, and bound his son Isaac and laid him on the altar, on top of the wood. Abraham stretched out his hand and took the knife to slay his son" (Genesis 22:9-10).

By now, the scene we are reading has also entered our imagination. We actually see, in slow motion, the elderly servant of God reaching for the weapon that will be used to follow through with the sacrifice. Is his hand shaking? Are tears forming in his eyes? This is the point in the story when we are frozen with fear and anticipation. Our hearts are racing as we see that knife lifted high above Abraham's head. We would close our eyes, but it would do no good, as we see that knife start to plummet toward precious Isaac.

But then...

> The angel of the LORD called to him from heaven and said, "Abraham, Abraham!" And he said, "Here I am." He said, "Do not stretch out your hand against the lad, and do nothing to him; for now I know that you fear God, since you have not withheld your son, your only son, from Me." Then Abraham raised his eyes and looked, and behold, behind him a ram caught in the thicket by his horns; and Abraham went and took the ram and offered him up for a burnt offering in the place of his son. (Genesis 22:11-13)

When the angel of the Lord presented Abraham with God's plan, a plan of great grace and wonder, Jesus was there! Jesus was right in the middle of the circumstance. Just as Jesus was present in the beginning, when the world was being formed and you were being formed, His presence is in the midst of your circumstance. If you look up to Him, He's there. And He's been there. Because He will never ask you to go anywhere He has not already been Himself.

When thinking about the places I have been, I remember, "Oh! Not only is He asking me to go there with Him, but He's already there." God accompanies us and He awaits our arrival.

Sacrificing Our Attitude

We discover, in this amazing story, how Abraham obediently sacrificed through his actions *and* through his attitude. God said to Abraham, "Since you have not held back from me or begrudged giving me your son, Abraham, I know that you fear Me." When I read this verse, it starts to work on my heart. It challenges me. Does it challenge you? You can push your circumstance out in front of Him and say, "Oh, go ahead, I know You're going to do what You will anyway, God." Or, you can offer it. Do not begrudge Him for asking for it; be willing to give it over.

Jehovah Jireh isn't your backup plan, He *is* your plan.

I believe that one of the most difficult offerings to make to God is grief. We hold on to the sadness and refuse to move forward. We begrudge Him because we want to bear the ache a bit longer, believing that if we do, it might turn into something else. Or maybe, given enough time, it will make more sense. Grief only turns to healing once we sacrifice it to God. When we offer it back to Him, He will provide peace. The attitude in which you offer something matters, and God honors it.

What is it in your life that you're begrudging God for doing? Would you be willing to offer it to Him? Offer Him your health instead of begrudging Him for requiring some of it. Offer Him your age instead of begrudging Him for the signs that go with aging. Offer Him your job, your family, your home, your finances, your singleness, your widowhood. Follow the example of Abraham—He did not begrudge but trusted.

As long as we are determined to provide for ourselves and self-protect, God can't provide. *Jehovah Jireh* isn't your backup plan, He *is* your plan. You can't make an offering of sacrifice to God by laying

Isaac *and* a ram on the altar together. God couldn't provide the ram until Abraham offered Isaac, and then God said, "No, I have something for you." And we have to give without knowing whether God will provide a substitution. We have to give without seeing beyond the moment's offering. We have to give with an attitude of humility and openness. This is how we prepare to receive all that *Jehovah Jireh* has for us.

Will you surrender it, your thing? Will you give it over to Him with a willing heart so you can then receive *Jehovah Jireh's* provision? Will you allow Him to give you joy in that place? Will you allow Him to accomplish what He wants to in and through you, even if you would rather not be in that place?

When we finally surrender our dreams and treasures and we trust God to provide, we realize His things are so much better. But first we have to let go. We have to release that stubborn, fearful, human grip on our circumstances and give it all to God. In the greatest crisis of my life, God provided. In Abraham's greatest crisis, God provided. Isaac and the ram were pointing to the cross and God's ultimate provision for sin. Hebrews says the blood of animals will not be adequate and the sacrifice of another life will not satisfy.

How many mothers think they can satisfy God on behalf of their children's lives? You might not literally try to lay yourself down, but you sacrifice yourself. God has told us that no other life can satisfy His requirement. *We* cannot satisfy the requirement; our sacrifice will never be enough. But God has provided all that is necessary, because He will only accept the perfect, holy, and the absolutely complete. He provided that in Jesus. "Behold, the Lamb of God who takes away the sin of the world!" (John 1:29).

The Ultimate Provision of Jesus

I was given such a clear picture of Jesus as my provision when I was on a group mission trip in Africa and we were faced with the daunting task of helping local schools, churches, and community health services to clean the streets of a dirty, dusty, remote town. Broken bottles, paper, tissue, and packaging wrappers were everywhere. If you can, imagine a place without trash receptacles, garbage services, or sewer and water drainage. Prior to our cleaning day, we rode through the town in our van thinking, *Why are we bothering to clean up? Won't it just return to the same bad condition as soon as we're done? Nothing can make a difference here.*

The day came for our project. In the heat, the smells and the tasks were offensive. In the moment, the work seemed so futile. And if we weren't already concerned, the people in charge warned us to be careful to avoid getting stuck by used needles that were often among the debris. Putting our fear and discouragement aside and pulling on the garden gloves we had brought with us, we started picking up trash. There was no rake or anything to scoop the trash, so we gathered it in piles to burn. Well, they didn't exactly burn, they smoldered. Again, I wondered what the point of it was.

At that moment, God gently opened my spiritual eyes and ears. He said, "Jan, this is a picture of the heart without Me. It's dirty and you don't know what to do with it or where to take your sin. Every once in a while, you try to sweep the sin up, to rid yourself of the trash, but it just smolders and still has an offensive odor in your life. I gave you Jesus so your heart can be clean. You don't ever have to wonder where to take the trash of your life. You don't have to hope that you can clean yourself up or succumb to a sense of pointlessness and purposelessness. Jesus is the perfect provision. He gave it all."

This clarity changed that service project for me. The dusty, dirty street became a sacred place of revelation. It transformed the picture of my heart and that of any person apart from Him. God made provision for all people; He has provided Jesus. He was *Jehovah Jireh* before any one of us knew what we needed. "God demonstrates His own love toward us, in that while we were still sinners, Christ died for us" (Romans 5:8 NKJV). Even back when I mistakenly thought provision came from the world, He already loved me and had provided Jesus. He prepared the answer before I knew how to call on His name. For me, He spared nothing.

Making Us Alive with Him

If you want to offend somebody, describe them as needy. Why? Because it's very humbling to see yourself as needy. Without thinking twice, we can make a reference like, "The needs of the people are great!" However, it is hard to say, "My needs are so great. My spiritual needs and my eternal needs are great." But in our heart we know this is true. So very true. And in the depth of that need, we meet the glory of *Jehovah Jireh*.

> When you were dead in your transgressions and the uncircumcision of your flesh, He made you alive together with Him, having forgiven us all our transgressions, having canceled out the certificate of debt consisting of decrees against us, which was hostile to us; and He has taken it out of the way, having nailed it to the cross. When He had disarmed the rulers and authorities, He made a public display of them, having triumphed over them through Him. (Colossians 2:13-15)

God lavishes His grace and love on us in times of greatest need. Where we are dead in our sin, He has made us alive together with Him. When I explored this verse and really took time to consider the spectacular significance of God's provision, I had to ask myself, *What part of my life am I refusing to surrender to Him, and therefore is not alive? What part of my life do I hold on to rather than giving it over to God in exchange for His life-giving provision?*

You can come to the cross, receive the free gift of salvation, and walk with God, but just like in Abraham's life, there can be a piece of your heart that you hold back. Abraham cherished his son. And like any devoted parent, he might have been inclined to place his child above his devotion to God. Therefore God tested Abraham so he would realize that he did ultimately love God even more than Isaac. He challenged Abraham to trust Him as the Resurrection and the Life.

When God provided the ram as a sacrifice to replace Isaac, Abraham met *Jehovah Jireh*. That thing that had plagued him became the experience through which Abraham would fully know God as Provider: "Abraham called the name of that place The Lord Will Provide, as it is said to this day, 'In the mount of the Lord it will be provided'" (Genesis 22:14).

What in your life needs to be given to God completely so that it can be raised back to newness of life? Are you offering a sacrifice that is pleasing to the Lord and which shows Him that you put Him above all else? Are you trusting that God is able to supply your every need? Are you looking to God to provide, or are you looking to the world to supply?

People, plans, and programs cannot fulfill our needs, but God can and does. The heart of Paul's overall message is: "My God shall supply the grace to carry you through. He will give you the strength to persevere. He gives life where there was only death. My God will give you all that you need."

God's supply is more than enough. He supplies all of your needs, not all of your wants or all of your wishes. *Jehovah Jireh* is not a study of "Jehovah Santa Claus," or "Jehovah Lottery," or "Jehovah Genie in a Bottle." *Jehovah Jireh* came to die on a cross. *Jehovah Jireh* was manifested in Jesus. *Jehovah Jireh*'s foremost concern is that your eternal needs would be provided for, and yes, because He is *Jehovah Jireh*, He also cares for your daily needs. What a gift it is to have the example of Abraham and God's relationship.

God walked every step of the way with Abraham. He walks every step of the way with you. As Abraham and Isaac were moving up one side of the mountain, God was moving the ram up the other side. Abraham couldn't see it, and neither could Isaac, but God's plan was in motion. The whole time we are walking our path, we only see the difficult path before us, but God views the big picture. He sees in advance all that He will do and provide from everlasting to everlasting. Not only that, but God knows how the journey, the offering, the mountain, and the struggle will be used in your life and for His purposes. As Abraham said to Isaac, "God will provide for Himself." The provision is ultimately for Himself, for His Glory, and for His eternal and everlasting purposes. Yet, when we are trusting of and secure in His provision, we receive a deep, spiritual contentment that can come from no other source.

> God climbed every part of Mount Moriah with Abraham and Isaac, and He will climb every step of the difficult path with you.

When Paul was writing to the Philippian church from prison, he did not use his letter to complain, seek empathy, or rant against his circumstances. Instead, he thanked the church for the gifts they had sent to him *and* he gave God glory through a remarkable attitude rooted in faith in God's provision and strength. Even as he sat in prison, his personal testimony shined: "I have learned to be content in whatever circumstances I am...I can do all things through Him who strengthens me" (Philippians 4:11,13).

Whether I have a lot or a little, whether I'm comfortable or uncomfortable, if my dreams come true or if they don't, if my ministry is thriving or struggling—I have learned that God is trustworthy. Where are you in your journey of trusting *Jehovah Jireh*? Can you say wholeheartedly these words from Paul: "My God will supply all your needs according to His riches in glory in Christ Jesus" (Philippians 4:19)? As you lift up the thing that weighs on you, speak this truth with hope: "My God shall supply."

God supplies according to His riches and glory. His resources are infinite. You don't have to understand it or explain it—it's beyond understanding—but you can trust His riches and glory because they are in Christ Jesus. He is complete, He is all things, and He is your all in all.

Encountering Jehovah Jireh

Trusting Jehovah Jireh

1. What burden do you carry in your life right now? When did it begin? How and why have you held back from surrendering this to the Lord? When you arise in the morning or lie down at night, are you concentrating on how difficult your life is, or are you focused on the One who is bigger and more powerful than the challenges you face? Before you even knew what your needs would be, Christ was provided as your supply. Rest in this today and see how it changes your heart and your perspective.

2. I shared about how God spoke to me of His grace through the image of the dirty streets in the African town. Do you believe that God has washed your heart clean? What image comes to your mind that helps you to see God as Provider and Savior? How has God already revealed Himself as Provider in your life?

Remembering the Benefits of Jehovah Jireh

1. When you lean on *Jehovah Jireh* for your supply, a remarkable benefit is that you live from a place of contentment rather than want. Your perspective changes. I encourage you to begin each day this week by reading aloud or praying this passage from Philippians. Ask God to make these words true in your own heart.

I have learned to be content in whatever circumstances I am. I know how to get along with humble means, and I also know how to live in prosperity; in any and every circumstance I have learned the secret of being filled and going hungry, both of having abundance and suffering need. I can do all things through Him who strengthens me. (Philippians 4:11-13)

2. Select one verse featured in the chapter or from your personal reading that is a reminder of the benefits of your Provider. Write it out so you can impress it upon your mind and heart.

Blessing Jehovah Jireh

1. God, as Provider, goes before us in our circumstances so that He can prepare the way and provide for our every need. You can bless *Jehovah Jireh* by releasing your anxiety or agitation about a future concern. Consider how this action then frees you to be content, to rest in God's supply, and to walk forward in the path God has prepared for you. Your obedience blesses God and, in turn, just like for Abraham, God blesses your journey.

2. Bless your Provider by sacrificing and surrendering your attitude and your perspective about a situation, a person, or a concern in your life. Actually, do this for *all* things in your life! When we give over our attitude to Him, we are letting go of the obstacles we create. Walk through this exercise with a humble heart, and you will be better able to serve Him and experience His abundance.

Praying to Jehovah Jireh

Father, I praise You and thank You for being Jehovah Jireh, my Provider. My salvation through the blood of Christ is the supply for me and for anyone who admits their need and looks to You, Lord. I stand in Your presence and trust You with my life, transgressions, dreams, family, future, pain, hope, and deepest need. I look to You and proclaim, "You are my Provider, Jehovah Jireh." I belong to You.

Thank You for Abraham's example, for showing me that You honor those who declare that You are forever God. I thank You, Jehovah Jireh, that You have met me here in my need. You have taken what was dead within me and given to me resurrection and life. In the name of the one You provided to take all of my sins, Jesus, the perfect Provision, I pray. Amen.

4

Experience Wholeness in *Jehovah Rophe*

God Is Your Healer

The trip out of Egypt was dramatic and traumatic for the Hebrew people. Some exits in life seem to be that way. The struggle and difficulty of life seems like it will never end and because it drags on and on with no end in sight, trial and trouble become the norm. In those circumstances it is easy to become resigned to the situation and begin to believe you have been forgotten or, even worse, abandoned while you struggle and strain to survive. Like me, you may have had a personal trial that persisted in varying degrees with prolonged intervals of pressure causing you to wonder if God had rejected your prayers or had even dismissed your cries for help. It may have been an illness or caring for someone who was sick, a relationship that was filled with tests and trials, or a constant roller coaster of emotional battles with depression, addiction, or abuse, to name just a few. Then one day, when you least expected it or had almost abandoned hope for things to ever be different, God stepped in and began to set His ordained change in motion.

Rearranged circumstances take some getting used to. Moses discovered this many times when God called him to the daunting task of delivering people who had been enslaved in Egypt for 400 hard years. His name, Moses, means "drawn out." Names have meanings, and we know God has called us by name before we were ever born. It is amazing to see the meaning of this baby boy's name fulfilled over and over throughout his lifetime. Baby Moses was literally drawn out of the water by Pharaoh's daughter after his mother hid him in a basket at the river's edge. He was drawn out of the palace and forced to run for his life after he murdered an Egyptian for abusing a Hebrew slave. While drawing water as a fugitive in Midian, he landed a wife! God drew him out of Midian 40 years later so he could draw the nation of Israel out of slavery under Pharaoh. Moses, as deliverer, constantly called God's people, Israel, to be drawn out from the other nations and be set apart. God's plans and purposes are accomplished through those who trust His great name.

Perfectly Timed Promises

When Moses least expected something to change, God showed up. In his early years, his identification as the adopted son of Pharaoh's daughter gave him power and influence. In indignation he murdered an Egyptian who was abusing and mistreating one of his own people, a Hebrew. His method and his timing to deliver his people was way off. Have you ever reacted apart from God's timing and God's method? It almost always makes matters worse, and it certainly did for Moses. Fearing for his life, he fled Egypt and went to Midian, where he lived as a shepherd of his father-in-law's flocks. Life settled in to a predictable existence for 40 years.

Perhaps you have settled in to a bearable and predictable life. It's not at all what you dreamed of, but you have resigned yourself to it. Take encouragement from the story of God's relationship with Moses. God was watching, waiting, and working all that time. While Moses was shepherding the flocks, God called him by name from a burning bush. He revealed Himself as God to Moses and reminded him of the commitment He had made with Abraham, Isaac, and Jacob to be their God. God never forgets His promises, and He never holds back from calling His people to walk in them. He told Moses: "I have surely seen the affliction of My people who are in Egypt, and have given heed to their cry…for I am aware of their sufferings. So I have come down to deliver them from the power of the Egyptians" (Exodus 3:7-8). Then God dropped one more important detail into this totally unexpected exchange: "Come now, and I will send you to Pharaoh, so that you may bring My people, the sons of Israel, out of Egypt" (v. 10).

Moses had lived for 40 years in exile in a foreign land because he tried to deliver his people apart from God's timing and method. Then God showed up and said, "It's time, and I'm using you." The young, passionate, hotheaded Moses felt capable and courageous enough to deliver his people in his own power. However, the older, wiser, humbled Moses wanted no part of the assignment. He knew he wasn't capable, he had no courage, and God certainly didn't need him. In my life I have noticed that God's assignments often come when I least expect them and when I've become comfortable with the way things are. He wants to do His work His way, and He will allow me to be His workman. God is not interested in me being comfortable. My resistance, objections, and excuses are all clear reminders of my keen sense of insufficiency.

Moses learned about God in so many new ways by stepping into a position he was inadequate and unprepared to take. I don't want my fears and insecurities to keep me from experiencing the supernatural power of His great name. How about you? What is God calling you to do that you are resisting and refusing? What promptings and nudges are tugging at the edges of your heart and mind right now? Do you sense God is saying to you, "Come now, I will send you"?

Maybe we both need to pray with belief, "God, You alone are

my source and supply. Apart from You, I cannot do anything!" Let's trust God to draw us out of our comfort zones so He can deliver us into His plans and promises.

God's Due Dates

The actual deliverance of the Israelites from Egypt was neither swift nor smooth. It took time and testing for Moses, the Hebrews, Pharaoh, and the Egyptians. Though God had promised deliverance, it would not be a cakewalk to victory. Chapters 7 through 14 of Exodus reveal the power of God, the rebellion of the human heart, and the tendency to allow doubt and fear to hold us captive even when God opens the door for us. In the physical realm, every parent knows delivery is not accomplished without grueling and intensive labor. That beautiful baby you finally hold is the result of strenuous and laborious work. The delivery is thrilling and exciting and exhausting. The same is true in the spiritual realm. For deliverance from the slavery of sin, we must believe in the promise of victory won on the cross and prepare our hearts, pray, wait, pray, obey, pray, engage in spiritual warfare, pray, and push through by faith!

Moses and the Israelites claimed God's deliverance when they walked through the Red Sea on dry land. They stood in amazement as they watched God roll the waves over the Egyptian army, killing every man, horse, and rider.

It was time for a celebration! They reveled in the power of God to destroy the enemy who pursued them relentlessly. They were free to serve the true and living God. God's deliverance is for His people, and His wonders and works are on behalf of those who trust and believe in Him, including you and me. When we are delivered from sin and become a child of God, we go from enslaved to free! And we, too, celebrate!

But then comes the matter of moving on, living a new life in a new land. For Moses it was to move the people on into the wilderness of Shur. "Sure about what?" might have been the question on every-one's mind. When you first became a believer, were you sure things would get easier in your life and your struggles would surely end? The Israelites definitely thought that. That is until "they went three days in the wilderness and found no water" (Exodus 15:22).

Forgetting God's Faithfulness

After all God had done for the Israelites during their exodus from Egypt, you would think that they would trust Him for each new trial. If He could part a sea of water and make a dry path through its midst, how hard could it be for God to make some water in the midst of the dry land? Yet fear has a way of chasing faith in God's goodness right out of our mind. The enemy tells you things weren't really that bad before. You actually start to recall the days under slavery and oppression as "the good ol' days." Have you ever had that experience after your own deliverance situations? Memory flees when you are threatened and uncertain. There have been times when I have prayed and waited and watched for God to move in my circumstances. When He opened or closed doors and made a way through the difficulty, I was filled with faith in His power to deliver. When the reality of the new place settled in and the needs for the present seemed overwhelming, I remembered the old days and old ways with fondness. I quickly forgot how desperately I wanted to be delivered from the burden and how painful the days were of watch-ing and waiting for God to move.

After traveling three days into the wilderness of Shur, the people were hot, tired, and thirsty. They arrived at Marah and found water and with it the hope that their thirst could be quenched and their bodies refreshed. But things were not what they seemed. When they tasted the waters at Marah, they were bitter and undrinkable. "The people complained against Moses, saying, 'What shall we drink?'" (Exodus 15:24 NKJV). I'm ashamed to admit, a little pressure in unfamiliar and uncertain territory can quickly reduce me to complaining too. I quickly forget that God has brought me this far and He will not abandon or forget me.

What has happened in your life that has not turned out to be what you thought it would? It could be a childhood experience or a relationship where you feel shortchanged. Maybe you said "for better or worse," but worse was not supposed to happen to you. Or maybe you took a job or changed your plans because you were presented with a better opportunity or a sweeter deal, only to discover it was an illusion or maybe an outright lie. The toll of these situations can cause us to forget God's faithfulness and become bitter.

A word to the wise: bitterness begins and spreads in quiet pools of the heart, like at Marah. The surface may appear to be sweet, but below that deceptive layer, the bitterness pollutes, contaminates, and eventually ruins all who make contact with it. The unhappiest people are those with spiritual depths polluted by unhealed hurts and deceptions. Many are sick physically and have tainted relationships throughout their lives. Bitterness is a deadly and dangerous spiritual wound, and it defiles many.

The Remedy for Bitterness

In the backlash of blame and the clamor of complaining, Moses knew where to turn for help. The need for water was legitimate, and His reaction to trouble was to cry out to God. The needs in your life right now may be desperate and legitimate. God is aware of the dangers and toils that lurk in the wilderness journey of life. Let's go back for a minute and think of the places where you have been disappointed, hurt, or wounded. The purpose is not to dredge up old feelings, but I know from personal experience that these places of bitterness don't simply go away when we bury them deep down and refuse to deal with them. Toleration of bitter pools compromises physical health, sours personal relationships, and contaminates spiritual life. Walk through these questions to see where bitterness might be brewing.

1. Have you become embittered toward God? Your thoughts may sound something like this: *Why did God let this injustice happen to me? If God loves me, why did He do this to me?*

2. Are you embittered toward another person(s)? Indicators are statements such as, "They are trying to ruin me. They are out to get me. They want to use me, misrepresent me. They never understand me."

3. Are you unwilling to let go of your own past sin, foolish choices, and painful consequences? You loathe yourself and the mess you have made of your life. This often is revealed in self-pity, selfishness, a critical spirit, and defensiveness.

If you see yourself in these, or you feel the draw toward bitterness in a current circumstance, it is time to seek the cure. The only cure.

Cry Out for the Cure

Like Moses, we must learn to cry out to God instead of complaining and blaming Him and others. "Then he cried out to the LORD, and the LORD showed him a tree; and he threw it into the waters, and the waters became sweet" (Exodus 15:25).

I love the things we see about our God here. *Jehovah Rophe* knows things about the hurting place we are in that we cannot know until He shows us. He is waiting for us to cry out to Him as our cure. Moses had never been in this wilderness before. The people had not left Egypt for more than 400 years. You have never been in this exact place before, but God knows everything you need to know. He knows the days ahead and all the challenges the future holds. Drinkable water was produced by casting the tree into the bitter pools. God's word provided the way.

> And He said, "If you will give earnest heed to the voice of the LORD your God, and do what is right in His sight, and give ear to His commandments, and keep all His statutes, I will put none of the diseases on you which I have put on the Egyptians; for I, the LORD, am your healer." (Exodus 15:26)

Jehovah Rophe is the "Lord who heals." His healing power is released into the bitter places in our lives when we listen to His voice and obey His truth. The Egyptians were plagued with disease and ruin because of refusal to listen to God's word spoken through Moses and blatant rebellion and disregard for His authority. *Jehovah Rophe* wants His people to know Him as the remedy for the sin-sick heart. We are all bent toward rebellion against His authority in our lives. He knows the need, and He knows the cure and has made provision for it. The sacred, blood-soaked cross of Christ is the tree of healing for all who will heed His voice and give ear to His command. "Whoever will call on the name of the LORD will be saved" (Romans 10:13). The cross is the source and solution that is able to turn ruined, bitter places of sin into sweet pools of grace.

Authentic Healing

Hundreds of years after the wilderness of Shur, Peter, an apostle and close companion to Jesus, wrote these words about Christ the Savior: "[Jesus] Himself bore our sins in His body on the cross, so that we might die to sin and live to righteousness; for by His wounds you were healed" (1 Peter 2:24). My rebellion and every place of bitter offense in my heart nailed Jesus to a tree, the cross. By listening to the call to repentance and crying for salvation in obedient faith, I now live an abundant and eternal life. *Jehovah Rophe* has healed my sins by His wounds! He gave me eternal healing for my soul. Praise to God whose love given through His only Son makes the way for me to have streams of living water flowing freely. Casting a tree into the bitter pool was an act of faith on Moses' part. When God showed him the tree, he didn't argue or demand an explanation. His response was humble obedience.

God always honors humble obedience to act on His word. He has shown us the Tree of Life. The cross of Christ is the power to cleanse, forgive, redeem, and reconcile us to God. The world offers all sorts of alternative cures for the deep longing in our soul. But God has "set eternity in the human heart" (Ecclesiastes 3:11 NIV). The reason there is no lasting satisfaction or genuine freedom from the pain and sorrow of life and the guilt and shame of sin is because there are no alternative remedies. Jesus said, "'I am the way, the truth, and the life. No one comes to the Father except through Me'" (John 14:6 NKJV).

> Jesus is The Way— Don't look elsewhere. The Truth— Trust and believe Me. The Life—Live in Me and give My life to others.

If alternatives have left you stranded in the wilderness, thirsting for life-giving water to refresh and sustain you, may I challenge you to take God at His word and cast the Tree of Life into your stagnant and contaminated heart. *Jehovah Rophe* is healer! He is able to heal bitter experiences, bitter people, and bitter circumstances.

Spiritual Healing Is God's Priority

If you are wondering why we have spent so much time on the subject of bitterness, it is because spiritual healing is *Jehovah Rophe's* priority. Heed the voice of the Lord given in clear instructions through the apostle Paul: "Let all bitterness and wrath and anger and clamor and slander be put away from you, along with all malice. Be kind to one another, tender-hearted, forgiving each other, just as God in Christ also has forgiven you" (Ephesians 4:31-32).

I can think of countless examples of people who are unwilling to heed these words. I am prayerfully sifting through my own heart to check for any unresolved places of bitterness as a result of being hurt, offended, or wronged. While the emotions may have some truth or validity to them, the emotion itself becomes toxic when we refuse to release the action and the person who offended. Left to itself, bitterness festers into rage and anger: "I hate...I refuse to speak...I will never forget..." Bitterness refuses kindness and compassion and withholds forgiveness from the other person while neglecting the forgiveness God has freely offered us. Marriages, families, generation to generation repeat the cycle. Look closely and you will almost always find physical infirmity and depleted health in the generations as well. I know a woman who suffers severe illnesses and chronic pain in her body due to many, many years of bitter complaining and relentless blaming. A close look at her life reveals a trail of individuals by whom she has been offended and harbored resentment and hatred toward. She will not speak to multiple people on her list of people who have wronged her. Her hypersensitivity and complaining taint and contaminate everything she does.

Once many years ago, I was given some helpful advice from a wise and godly mentor: "Do not receive the offense." When something hurtful is said or done, this is one of my first prayers: "Lord, help me not to be easily offended and overly sensitive. Don't let the thoughtlessness or carelessness of others cause me to struggle and strive with You or them. Help me remember the times I have been offensive to others and most of all to You. Keep me mindful of Your forgiveness and freedom from guilt and shame. By Your power I choose to forgive the person who has hurt me."

I'm not saying I get there immediately or easily. I have had serious sessions of wrestling with the offense and being tempted to hold on to the wrong. It's crazy how good it feels in the moment to hash through the gory details and rehearse the words and actions over and over again. For the moment it seems empowering to enlighten others. Even now there is one offense that comes to my mind that I would really like to tell you about. The only point of doing it would be so you would join me in saying, "That is the most callous and hateful thing I have ever heard." So see, I still need to cast the tree into my puddles of bitterness. I'm desperate to guard and protect my heart with the healing that only Jesus can give.

What About Physical Healing?

You may have opened this chapter because you want to understand God's willingness to provide physical healing for you or someone you love. The question on the tip of your tongue is, "Does *Jehovah Rophe* heal physical illnesses, pain, and infirmities today?" We know of many times throughout the Gospels when Jesus healed people of disease, fevers, hemorrhaging, and many other physical, mental, and emotional maladies. Jesus, the Great Physician, knows what the symptoms indicate and what the source of the illness is, and He is the cure. Remember the example of the bleeding woman.

> A woman who had been suffering from a hemorrhage for twelve years, came up behind Him and touched the fringe of His cloak; for she was saying to herself, "If I only touch His garment, I will get well." But Jesus turning and seeing her said, "Daughter, take courage; your faith has made you well." At once the woman was made well. (Matthew 9:20-22)

This example has encouraged me to continue to pursue His healing power and reach to touch His garment many times over the last few years. For me, the slow and steady drain from my heart and mind, affecting my physical strength and energy, was rooted in grief and sorrow. In 2010, my only son, James, died suddenly while living and working in Africa. Although sadness and sorrow tried to utterly debilitate me, I knew that the Great Physician would honor my faith as long as I would reach toward Him. My healing came when I crawled into His presence and lifted my weak and trembling hand in His direction. When my voice was too weak to cry out, He read my heart cry and knew my need. I asked Him to help me guard my heart from being offended by the way He had chosen to work in my life. He has indeed made me well, and today I live with a renewed sense of joy and increased strength. I join with David in Psalm 30:2, "O Lord my God, I cried to you for help, and You healed me." *Jehovah Rophe* is my Healer!

On the edge of collapse, a friend's tests and evaluations eventually revealed a rare form of blood cancer. While the doctor explained the seriousness of his findings and began to outline treatment options, she felt a clear impression in her spirit. The still, small voice of God spoke His Word to her, "This sickness is not unto death, but for the glory of God, that the Son of God might be glorified through it" (John 11:4 nkjv). With no thread of hope apart from the promise God gave her at her diagnosis, she has endured grueling treatments. God has given her countless opportunities to glorify Him. She continues to thrive in spite of leukemia. She says, "My body has evidence of disease, but I am healed by faith." Like many of you, I have heard testimonies of physical healing that cannot be explained from a medical standpoint. I believe them all because I know my God is able. "I am the Lord…is there anything too hard for Me?" (Jeremiah 32:27 nkjv).

I have also watched many faith-filled, God-honoring people die as a result of physical disease and sickness. I share this truth to encourage you as you seek and pray for healing. Sin is spiritual sickness, and it is always lethal. Sin will never, ever bear fruit. However, physical sickness can be used to bear much fruit. In times of great suffering, God is often acknowledged and praised as the only source of hope and healing. When situations are dire and the prognosis is death, we are more willing to release the temporary and give our full attention to the eternal. When we are weak, frail, and our body is failing, there is a deep need for the grace and strength of God. His power is on display in our weakness. His glory is revealed. Some of the most spiritually powerful people I have ever known are sick, living their days in chronic pain, and are feeble and frail in body. I think of a friend of mine who has been battling ovarian cancer for 11 years. Her sick bed is not a pool of bitterness where complaining and resentment are stored. Each day is received as a gift from God, and she lives for His glory. Her life is fruitful and productive, a testimony to the verse, "Though our outer man is decaying, yet our inner man is being renewed day by day" (2 Corinthians 4:16). I pray for her and join with many others in asking God to heal her. He is able. He is Sovereign God, and He has plans and purposes that are beyond my understanding. I trust Him, and my friend's trust in Jesus helps my faith grow stronger and deeper.

If you are sick and your body is failing, will you cast the Tree of Life into the pool of bitterness and trust God's power to make these days sweet in His sight and purposeful for eternity? Will you apply the healing power of His Word and believe He is able to restore your health if that is His will? My young friend Brady struggled with addiction for many years. One day he shared with me that he had decided to take God's Word literally. He took Psalm 107:20 and applied it to his own personal place of vulnerability and weakness: "He sent His word and healed them, and delivered them from their destructions." He said, "I took the Word like meds. Three times a day I read—I ate—words of life and believed they had the power to heal my convoluted thinking and my sins." Today he is walking in freedom and sharing the healing power of God's Word with others. When my friend Karen's husband died after a valiant and painful battle with lymphoma, her response to a condolence offered was, "God won the battle with cancer. Ron is completely healed and alive in the presence of the Lord." That's a testimony of sickness bearing eternal fruit!

❧❧❧

It is never too late, too hard, or too much for
Jehovah Rophe to heal a sin-sick heart.

Drinking Sweet, Living Water

One day a tired and travel-weary Jesus stopped at a water well in Samaria. He asked a woman who came to draw water in the middle of the day to give Him a drink. A conversation ensued that led Jesus to challenge her to drink after Him. "If you knew the gift of God, and who it is who says to you, 'Give me a drink,' you would have asked Him, and He would have given you living water" (John 4:10). The Samaritan woman learned that Jesus was indeed present to perform healing in her sin-sick body, and she gladly drank after Him. But she wasn't content to drink only for herself—she wanted to share the cup of living water with everyone she knew! That's the effect spiritual healing has on us. It's contagious.

I'll never forget the day I drank living water. I was a young adult whose spiritual thirst was not being quenched by religion, good works, or even a "comfortable" life. I was parched deep within and finally, someone offered me living water. Everything changed when I drank the life of Jesus and He became a well within me springing up into everlasting life. Now I want to remind you that Jesus is present to perform healing in your life. It is never too late, too hard, or too much for Him to heal a sin-sick heart.

Perhaps meeting *Jehovah Rophe* as the Lord Who Heals has spoken to some place deep within your heart. This could be the first time you have ever identified your complaints and discontent with circumstances and people in your life as ailments of your spirit that need to be healed. If life has felt like a wilderness journey into one disappointing and misleading place after another, this is your time to listen to God's voice and take action on what He shows you to do. Instead of a weary, wandering spirit, we can walk with Him through the wildernesses and trust Him to use each place to demonstrate the power of His great name.

Encountering Jehovah Rophe

Trusting Jehovah Rophe

1. What do your attitudes about disappointing, unpleasant places in your life reveal about the condition of your heart? Have you been able to identify any places in need of supernatural healing? If so, name them to *Jehovah Rophe*.

2. Can you identify where bitterness in your heart has caused trouble for others in your life? Remember guilt is not God's tool. The enemy wants you to remain embittered and stagnant, but God wants to reveal His truth so He can perform healing in your life and those lives you may have tainted. "The goodness of God leads you to repentance" (Romans 2:4 nkjv). Pray to trust His goodness. *I humbly ask You,* Jehovah Rophe, *to forgive my bitter tongue, attitude, and actions. I know I have hurt*

   _____.

   You have the power to heal the wounds inflicted. I plead Your healing touch in my relationship(s) with _____.
   Please guide me and minister healing in my heart. Amen.

Remembering the Benefits of Jehovah Rophe

1. Knowing *Jehovah Rophe* gives us tremendous hope when we find ourselves in unanticipated and unpleasant places. He offers to release us from the life-choking complications created by chronic complaints, a critical and resentful spirit, and casting blame and shame on others. Call to Him in faith and ask Him to come to the pools of disappointment and desperation. Release His healing into your heart. You can be made well!

2. By choosing to clean out the refuse and debris in our heart, the waters are freed to flow and offer the sweet refreshment found in Jesus. As you read and soak on the truth of these words, I pray this will become the deepest desire of your heart.

> Now on the last day, the great day of the feast, Jesus stood and cried out, saying, "If anyone is thirsty, let him come to Me and drink. He who believes in Me, as the Scripture said, 'From his innermost being will flow rivers of living water.'" (John 7:37-38)

Blessing Jehovah Rophe

1. *Jehovah Rophe* is blessed when the lives of His people reflect the healing power of His name. One practical way we can do this is to learn to not be easily offended by others or by Him. John the Baptist devoted his life to preparing the way for the Messiah to come. He was faithful to his call and yet found himself imprisoned because of Herod's bitter and vengeful wife. While imprisoned, he sent word to Jesus, asking Him, "Are you the Expected One?" Jesus answered, "Go and report to John what you have seen and heard...Blessed is he who does not take offense at me" (Luke 7:22-23). When life doesn't seem fair, we need to take encouragement from Jesus and not be offended by the way He chooses to work in our life. The blessings of being unoffended are eternal. Will you allow His word to be enough for now?

2. If you or someone you love is suffering physically, would you be willing to ask *Jehovah Rophe* to take the sickness and supernaturally use it to bear eternal fruit? Common sense and laws of nature say it is impossible for a sick tree to produce a bountiful yield. But the healing touch of *Jehovah Rophe* is able to produce glorious, divine, sweet, eternal fruit.

Praying to Jehovah Rophe

Father, thank You for revealing Yourself to Moses and now to me as Jehovah Rophe, *my Healer. You have given me the Tree of Life through the cross of Christ, and by His stripes I am healed. Your touch has the power to make bitter waters places of sweet blessing. Thank You for delivering me and giving me the opportunity to flow with rivers of living water. I lift up Your name over every wounded and broken place in my heart and ask for the cross of Christ to cleanse and cure me. By faith in Your name,* Jehovah Rophe, *I believe every place of sickness and infirmity in my body, mind, and spirit can become a place of bountiful eternal fruit. In Jesus' name. Amen.*

5

Walk in Victory with *Jehovah Nissi*

God Is Your Banner

lmost every weekend, people gather across the globe to cheer their team to victory. They wear team colors, wave flags, and proudly demonstrate loyalty and allegiance. The fans identify with the team, and the team relies on its fans.

The Israelites were not playing sports in the wilderness, but they were about to experience the threat of opposition against well-trained warriors. They would also experience the power of God's unwavering loyalty and supernatural support during fierce battle. They met and defeated God's enemy, Amalek, and Moses built an altar and called it *Jehovah Nissi*, "The LORD is My Banner" (Exodus 17:15).

Their preparation for this epic confrontation was unprecedented. They were unprepared and unqualified in every way to experience victory. Discomfort in the wilderness had led to a deep divide between the people of Israel and Moses their leader. Physical circumstances caused discouragement and doubt, murmuring and complaining, faultfinding and blaming. All are habit forming. The people were perfecting the art of being miserable at every stop in the wilderness.

Are you in a wilderness place in your life? Are the circumstances and conditions a breeding ground for a complaining spirit? Beware: Attitudes influence perspective, and the enemy is lurking and waiting for our focus to be on our trouble instead of our victory. When we become self-absorbed and preoccupied, our places of vulnerability are exposed with complaints. The enemy's strategy is to prevent advancement through your personal wilderness.

Facing the Enemy

The Amalekites were descendants of Esau, the brother who sold his birthright for a bowl of stew. Esau and Jacob represent two opposing attitudes toward the God of their father, Isaac. Esau and his generations were enemies to God, while Jacob's descendants became the chosen nation of Israel. They would be in direct opposition to one another from generation to generation.

Esau's appetites and cravings for immediate gratification are characteristics of the sin nature in all of us. Scripture often refers to the struggle between the flesh and the Spirit. "For the flesh desires what is contrary to the Spirit, and the Spirit what is contrary to the flesh. They are in conflict with each other, so that you are not to do whatever you want" (Galatians 5:17 NIV). Each time the Israelites met discomfort and challenge, their flesh cried for the ease of Egypt, in spite of God's ever-present help. While focusing on the desires of their flesh, their spiritual well-being was vulnerable to the enemy.

My own faith journey has been through some rich and fruitful places, along with stretches in life where circumstances left me dry and desolate. The temptation during difficulties is to forget the constant presence of God's faithful watch over me. When my spirit lags and my focus is inward, I am quick to lament my losses. This is the constant battle between flesh and spirit, temporal and eternal, or Amalek versus Israel.

Our discontent often leaves the door wide open
for deceit and destruction.

Ultimately, Amalek represents the enemy of the cross and preys on followers to this day. He is present in every generation. Those who have no regard for the Lord are allied with Amalek. Moses declared, "The LORD is My Banner" as he erected an altar to honor God's victory.

Remember the Israelites weren't warriors—they were a ragtag group of former slaves who weren't sure where they were going. They had no training or weapons, they weren't prepared, and they didn't know tactical logistics. However, they had the only thing necessary: *Jehovah Nissi* was in their midst, and He was present to fight for them.

Dependent on God's Victory

Scripture refers to believers as strangers and aliens in this world. We are called to be different from the world we live in. We might not be welcomed or accepted by those we encounter. This is a characteristic of our faith journey, and it might very well be a part of your personal wilderness experience right now. Maybe you have been wandering and doubting and looking back at your glory days when you had fewer troubles. While clouds of discontent alter your perspective, the enemy is circling to attack your area of weakness, whatever it may be: pride, doubt, weariness, temptation, apathy, anger, self-pity, or faithlessness. Our discontent often leaves the door wide open for deceit and destruction.

Your Amalek will come. The only way to withstand his attack is to shift your focus from self to God. He is the one who gives us victory. This is something we would know beyond a doubt if only we would remember how often He has brought us through our wilderness experiences. There were countless times when God intervened on Israel's behalf. Often when we don't deserve it, God delivers us, and the victory belongs to Him.

When the Israelites, motley crew that they were, triumphed over the Amalekites, it was God's victory. He used those who were committed to Him to make it happen. Those who were obedient followed God's leading. Moses instructed Joshua to go into battle, and then he went to the top of a hill to pray over the battle. He held the staff of God in his hand as a symbol of God's personal and powerful involvement in the battle.

> Joshua did as Moses told him, and fought against Amalek; and Moses, Aaron, and Hur went up to the top of the hill. So it came about when Moses held his hand up, that Israel prevailed, and when he let his hand down, Amalek prevailed. But Moses' hands were heavy. Then they took a stone and put it under him, and he sat on it; and Aaron and Hur supported his hands, one on one side and one on the other. Thus his hands were steady until the sun set. So Joshua overwhelmed Amalek and his people with the edge of the sword. (Exodus 17:10-13)

They were obedient, prayerful, and their faith in God's powerful presence in battle allowed Israel to prevail against Amalek. When the fighting was over and the Israelites had won, God spoke to Moses with harsh language about Amalek: "Write this in a book as a memorial and recite it to Joshua, that I will utterly blot out the memory of Amalek from under heaven" (Exodus 17:14-15). This seems so extreme. But even with these instructions, God had a plan for good, encouragement, and to lay the groundwork for future victories for His people.

After all the complaining the Israelites had done before the battle, is it any wonder that God wanted this victory to be marked for all time? He did not want any of the people present or future generations to forget this victory over evil was won in His name and in His power. Yes, this moment in their history was that important. And God wanted Moses to share it with Joshua so he would be reminded of God's faithfulness and strength. God was absolutely intolerant toward Amalek because God leaves no loopholes for those who do not fear Him. Amalek's attack on the Israelites was an attack on God.

Can you recall times God has delivered you from darkness into light and given you a future and hope? Have you built an altar because He is the God who has healed sin in your life, the God who has revealed places where a bitter root wanted to take hold and defile many? His finished work on the cross secures eternal life for you. Would you build an altar to declare, "I submit myself anew. Apart from *Jehovah Nissi*, I would have died in the wilderness."

When we build an altar to the Lord in honor of our victory in Him, we tell the world and future generations those moments of overcoming are because *Jehovah Nissi* fought our battles for us.

Where the Real Battles Take Place

So how does knowing *Jehovah Nissi* impact our lives? We're not engaged in physical battles like the Israelites were, but we are engaged in spiritual battles. If you are a believer, you are in the war. When you're born again and the life of Christ comes to indwell your life, you have become an enemy to the enemy of your soul. He hates Jesus in you, and his strategy is to do everything to take Him off the throne of your life.

I know to some people this probably sounds rather extreme. "I'm in a war? There's a battle, and I'm supposed to get all involved in this? What happened to peaceful, quiet Christians who don't engage?" The truth is the Christian life is extreme, and you really can't afford to be a clueless Christian. This world is a war zone, and spiritual failure will be absolutely unavoidable because ambushes are set against you on the path every single day unless you are spiritually attentive and alert.

David, who was a mighty warrior and fought battle after battle in the name of God, said to God, "You have given a banner to those who fear you, that it may be displayed because of the truth" (Psalm 60:4). God-fearing people are those who take the Word of God seriously. They don't play church. They don't simply go through the motions of being religious; they own up, they stand up, and they raise the banner of *Jehovah Nissi* over their lives for all to see. They display their loyalty and allegiance to Him.

I think of all of the years that I went to church, and yet I was clueless. No one ever told me there was a battle; no one ever told me there was an enemy that wanted to discourage me, knock me off my path, and take me out of God's will. I didn't know anything—I was a powerless Christian. It took the truth of God's Word and the Holy Spirit's revelation for me to awaken to the battles that circled my life and me.

Would you ask God to open spiritual eyes so that you can see what the true battle is in your life? Let's take marriage for example. Marriage was God's idea; it was God's plan. It's His picture of Christ and His love for the church, His bride. Strife in your marriage is the enemy's attack against Jesus in you, to ruin your marriage. Maybe you think the battle is with your children or an addiction? It's easy to point to these people or problems because they present themselves in the natural world. We need God to give us spiritual eyes to clearly see the actual battle and where it's coming from. "For our struggle is not against flesh and blood, but against the rulers, against the authorities, against the powers of this dark world against the spiritual forces of evil in the heavenly realms" (Ephesians 6:12).

Would you ask Him to give you spiritual ears to recognize and discern the lies of the enemy? Jesus said, "He is a liar and the father of lies" (John 8:44). The enemy, Amalek, whispers "God didn't hear your prayers; you're not really making a difference in your family. Jesus didn't really come through for you in that situation, did He?

Why are you sick? Why are you divorced? Why did you fail out of that class? Why is your job gone? Where is God in your life?" The enemy is planting lies so that he can begin to undermine your confidence in Christ Jesus, and so that you will complain against Him. In Psalm 20:5, David said, "We will rejoice in your salvation, and in the name of our God we will set up our banners" (NKJV). Counterattack the enemy by rejoicing in your salvation. How can you be quiet and passive and worry about offending someone by identifying with Jesus? He has set His banner over you. We are called to support, be loyal to, and identify with *Jehovah Nissi*. Rejoicing is a powerful weapon of spiritual warfare.

When you meet the believers in Africa, they want you to know the most important part of their identity right away. Immediately after they tell you their name, they claim their status as a believer in the Lord Jesus Christ. It is who they are, and they rejoice in it. They want you to know whose they are and they identify under the banner of His great name. There, it is accepted and expected for me to say, "I am Jan Harrison. I am born again and saved by the blood of Christ. I'm a mother, and I'm married to Frank, and this is what I do and this is who I am."

The banner of *Jehovah Nissi* has been raised over my household and me. When James passed away, the enemy's attack was intense. The battle was great, and the enemy circled to destroy our faith, hope, future, family, and testimony. People would ask, "Where was God? Why didn't He protect your family? " The enemy wanted us to say, "We're done. It's over. The cost is too high. The battle is so hard. It's not worth it. We can't go on in faith." The enemy wanted us to focus on loss and become self-absorbed in sorrow and grief. It was a temptation. But Jesus waved His victory banner over us; He identified with us and was our advocate against the enemy.

Moses had Aaron and Hur to hold up his hands in prayer. You and I have an advocate with the Father. When you are tired, when you are weary, when the battle is difficult, when the depths are great, Jesus, your High Priest, is praying for you. Other believers in the body of Christ come alongside and hold you up before the throne of grace. Wouldn't we all want to be identified with a group like that? Why would you want to be isolated and disconnected from His presence? *Jehovah Nissi* is your banner. He gives us victory step-by-step, day-by-day, year-by-year, until we see Him face to face.

Until that day, build an altar and declare before heaven and earth, "The Lord is my Banner."

Where We Are Most Vulnerable

The enemy of God comes from three places in your life. The first is from your flesh. Your emotions and feelings, cravings and desires mislead and misguide you and take you off course. The enemy will take advantage of times when you feel sorry for yourself, complain, and allow self-pity to consume you. Jesus gave specific warnings to His disciples about this very thing. These were the men who followed Him, loved Him, and understood to the best of their ability His mission. They wanted to be identified with Him and called His own. Jesus knew even earnest followers needed to hear His words of caution, "Keep watching and praying that you may not enter into temptation; the spirit is willing, but the flesh is weak" (Matthew 26:41).

The second place the enemy comes from is the world. God tells us that we are either for Him or against Him and the whole world lies under the sway, or the influence, of the wicked one. There's no neutral territory. Clueless Christians want to believe there's neutral territory— they want to walk down la-la-land's path without getting too deep in spiritual understanding and conviction. That's the enemy's deception. He is waiting to ambush you. We are most vulnerable when we naively believe that we only need to avoid what is overt and obviously evil. Seedy and dirty is easy to identify. But, my friend, don't we know there are many subtle dangers and pitfalls in our world? Perspectives and agendas presented as truth in the media, culturally acceptable actions or choices that seem harmless yet undermine godly conviction, and entertainment that erodes the boundaries we set forth to preserve our purity and our focus. This is a small representation of outlets that tell us what our priorities need to be, what we deserve, what we are owed, what other people owe us, and what our worth is. They are all part of the enemy's attack to keep us knocked off balance, to take Christ off the throne of our lives, and to oppose Jesus in us.

The third area we encounter the enemy of God is when we directly encounter the devil. "Be of sober spirit, be on the alert. Your adversary, the devil, prowls around like a roaring lion, seeking someone to devour" (1 Peter 5:8). The devil doesn't want to do a taste test with you—he wants to devour you. He wants to chew you, tear you, and shred you. Am I exaggerating? It is true! He wants to make your life a bloody mess. We are living in a war zone, and every single step is a potential land mine. What are we supposed to do about all that? Look at Jude's plea with believers exposed to false teachings and other threats to the faith: "Beloved, while I was making every effort to write you about our common salvation, I felt the necessity to write to you appealing that you contend earnestly for the faith which was once for all handed down to the saints" (Jude 1:3). Jude felt the urgency to spark awareness in believers to hold fast and fight for the faith. This message is our call.

Actions of a Contender

If you're a contender, you're going after the reward. If you're a contender for a title in a tennis match, then you have skills and abilities and you are going for victory. You're in a competition, you're engaging, and your aim is to win. This is the commitment and passion that compels us to be identified with *Jehovah Nissi*. Because He is the reward, we are not going to allow anyone or anything to steal our victory. We must train for the prize.

Jesus won the ultimate victory on the cross, but until we get to heaven, and until we stand in His presence, you and I must contend for the faith. Jude wrote the letter because false teachers were undermining the gospel. Today, there are false teachers trying to water down, shake apart, dilute, cut, and paste the truth. They were trying to make God's Word fit culture. In the heat of the battle for truth, we might be tempted to run and hide (that's the flesh leading!). Spectators are not contenders! We must stand and contend. We're called to engage. Jesus engaged! He went to the cross. Jesus took your sin and my sin. He took the wickedness and the evil and the sin of the world and was nailed to a cross. He engaged! He descended into hell, the Father turned His back on Him, and He felt the pain. He engaged in order to secure our victory by coming out of the tomb on the third day. So how is it that we contend for the faith?

Spectators are not contenders! We must stand and contend. We're called to engage. Jesus engaged!

Know the truth and obey it. James said, "Be a hearer and a doer of the word" (James 1:22, paraphrase). Don't keep going to church or doing Bible study week after week and not allow it to make a difference. Words of life should change you and your priorities, ideals, principles, and actions. They should change the very person you are. Confront and guard against false teaching. Contending is nonstop.

Are you willing to stand valiantly for the power of the gospel in your family, workplace, church, and any place where you have a sphere of influence? The name of Jesus is offensive. Here is a good example: When asked to pray in a group, some will request that you not pray in Jesus' name. They do not care if you pray in anybody else's name. There is power in His name. His name will make the devil run. Jesus is the name the enemy hates. You and I must contend for the gospel and the truth—the whole truth—and we must not back down.

Pray and pray some more. Moses lifted up his hands to pray throughout the Israelites' battle with the Amalekites, and he needed help. You and I can't hold our hands up for long without help. Thanks to Jesus, we don't have to. In Jesus, we have a High Priest. He's seated. His work is done. He's seated next to the Father, praying on your behalf right now. As a part of the body of Christ, prayer is a powerful benefit of belonging to *Jehovah Nissi*.

Wave the banner of *Jehovah Nissi* and make Him
the rallying point in your life. You may lose a few
skirmishes, but the final victory has been won.

Paul gave us wise counsel concerning prayer: "Rejoice always; pray without ceasing; in everything give thanks; for this is God's will for you in Christ Jesus" (1 Thessalonians 5:16-18). "With all prayer and petition pray at all times in the Spirit" (Ephesians 6:18). Pray without ceasing and pray in the Spirit. When you are a contender, your spirit is lined up with His spirit and your life is saturated with the Word of God. Jesus told His disciples, "If you abide in Me, and My words abide in you, ask whatever you wish, and it will be done for you" (John 15:7). This is possible when we are abiding in the vine, praying in His Spirit, and following the guidance of the Holy Spirit. God goes to work on our behalf if we lay our agendas down and lift up His name, telling Him, "I'll do whatever you ask me to do, Lord. Show me." This is our call to action as contenders, my friend.

Prayer Warriors in Battle

I've never seen people pray like the people at Namanga Baptist Church pray. They're a little Christian church surrounded by mosques. Five times a day, the Muslim call to prayer is broadcast over loud speakers. During Ramadan, the chanting and praying last all day long. When the Namanga members enter the small compound around their church, there are people trying to intimidate them by spitting and shaking their fists. The Christian prayer warriors are strangers in the land they call home.

When you are a stranger and unaccepted in your own land, you learn to lean into *Jehovah Nissi* for strength and victory. Chances are most of us have not been threatened or endangered by simply going to church. You must decide how high you will hold your banner. These believers contend for their faith and recognize the desperate need for *Jehovah Nissi* to unfurl His banner over them. Rather than complain or blame God for placing them in this difficult environment, they weep and cry out in prayer for their neighbors all around them. They climb "prayer mountain" and look out over their city and see it as a spiritual battlefield. They're not mad at a girl for spitting at them. They don't resent the Muslims who refuse to let them into businesses and shops. They know the battle isn't against people—it is a battle against the knowledge of God.

In faith, they ask God to raise His standard over them and put the enemy on notice. "This camp belongs to the true and living God." *Jehovah Nissi* is in their midst. They stand on the frontline and contend against the enemy for their community. They ask for the kingdom of God to come, for a sweeping wind of revival and the Spirit to move through their town. The believers know if they don't stand on the truth of God and pray, the enemy will come like a flood. They will be shut out, and in this case, Sharia law will become the law of the land, and they will be martyred for their identity in Christ. That's a picture of what it means to contend!

As contenders, we need to pray for eyes to see the battle and to recognize what's coming against us through the culture: the delusion, the lies, and everything that wants to eliminate the cause of Christ. Are you ready? Do you know and obey the Word and allow it to make a difference in your life? Ask for spiritual eyes to see and spiritual ears to hear so you recognize God's truth from Satan's lies. Wave the banner of *Jehovah Nissi* and make Him the rallying point in your life. You may lose a few skirmishes, but the final victory has been won. *Jehovah Nissi* is praying and guarding over you. Who can condemn you if His banner is over you?

Encountering Jehovah Nissi

Trusting Jehovah Nissi

1. What battle are you aware of in your life right now? Ask God for spiritual eyes and ears so that you understand the scope of it and the source of it. Ask with expectation that you will receive clarity. Pray for *Jehovah Nissi* to help you eliminate the source or strengthen you for battle.

2. Which enemies or lies are you trusting instead of the Word of *Jehovah Nissi*? Think through the adversaries we explored: your flesh, the world and its false teachings, and the devil. Surrender your ties to any of these and turn your attention and praise to *Jehovah Nissi*.

Remembering the Benefits of Jehovah Nissi

1. Think of times when *Jehovah Nissi* has gone to battle for you. Maybe it happened through a friend or a change of circumstance. Maybe you have witnessed hearts changed and obstacles cleared. There are many battles. And *Jehovah Nissi* is the one to stand up for you and stand with you. Reflect on your journey and claim those times you experienced victory in *Jehovah Nissi*.

2. Look back over your life and think about the battles and the victories, big and small. Write these down in your journal, and take time to praise God for bringing you through so many circumstances. Not only will you draw closer to the heart of *Jehovah Nissi*, but your heart will be strengthened

and encouraged for anything you face now. Hold on to your Victor's benefits.

Blessing Jehovah Nissi

1. God, as our Victor, does not leave us behind and unprotected. What battle is going on in your life right now that you have stepped away from because of fear? Name it. Then shed that timidity and step forth in the power of *Jehovah Nissi*. Bless Him by raising your banner, your voice, and your awareness so that you are a true contender. And when that victory comes, write it down and create an altar of tribute in some way so that you do not forget that God was and is with you.

2. When I think of the strength and faithfulness of the people of Namanga, I am humbled. My weakness and need for victory through *Jehovah Nissi* is never more evident. When have you had a real-life example of others resting in the might of the Lord as their banner? Reflect on that now. Give thanks to *Jehovah Nissi* and bless Him with deep gratitude for this model of leaning in to His strength. Now follow that example with renewed conviction!

Praying to Jehovah Nissi

Jehovah Nissi, *I thank You that the victory is in Jesus. Give me eyes to see this victory in a new way for my daily life. I confess that I have not always contended for the faith. Forgive me for being too worried about what others think, or too scared of the enemy to realize that You are with me. I praise You for Your unchanging Word and for the freedom I have to study it and be taught by Your Spirit so that I may recognize the truth. Lord, I pray that You will go before me and before each person in Your army. Help each of us to be alert, wise, and certain of the strategies of warfare that You have given us in Your Word and through prayer. It's under the mighty and matchless name of Jesus that I submit myself today and gladly give to You my loyalty and my allegiance. Amen.*

6

Live Fearlessly with *Jehovah Shalom*

God Is Your Peace

Shalom! This Hebrew greeting means "peace." How wonderful to welcome one another with an expression of peace. In our hurried lives, our greetings and our exit lines tend to be as rushed as we are. I think this is true in human relationships and often in our relationship with God. Busyness and preoccupation with things of the world tend to push out the peace and amp up the anxiety. How much peace do you have today?

Maybe there is something or someone that has been gnawing away at your peace. Maybe it's a decision or a deadline that's causing your heart to race. Many of us have an issue in our life that we have absolutely no ability to change and it causes us fear. When you review your list of peace-stealers, do you realize the same issues present themselves over and over? It's amazing how the same old problems can nip at our heels and cause us to toss and turn, bite our nails, and spiral into the pit of defeat.

How have we not gained control over them? We're smart, right? We have faith and ability, and we have minds that can, at least usually, discern the difference between troubles that merit concern and those that are blown out of proportion. Yet, we end up with the same list and often the same unhealthy behaviors to try and deal with that list, all because our peace is under assault. The enemy is anxious to steal our peace.

The more I think about it, the more I understand how peace is a hard-fought battle. It is not something that just happens, though many of us tell ourselves that if just the right circumstances are in place, the peace will come. We think tranquil places void of distracting sounds will provide peace. We have blamed our messy kitchen cupboards for the anxiousness that plagues us. And when the demands of family pull us in too many directions, we are sure that a spa with flute music playing in the background is our pass to inner peace. But those ideas are based on the belief that peace is the absence of conflict. And that is not true. Jesus lived, was nailed to a cross, and suffered until His death. Christ fought hard to secure our peace, and now we have to fight hard to hold on to that peace. We have to be intentional and have our spirits engaged so that we can pursue God's peace even when the enemy tries to steal it.

This is when we don't just use *shalom* as a welcome of peace, but we actually welcome *Jehovah Shalom*, "The Lord Is Our Peace," into our circumstances.

Eventually, and quite possibly often, something or someone will threaten to steal the peace of God in your life. You have to be strategic. You have to be purposeful, deliberate, and tactical about how to remain in God's peace in spite of your everyday circumstances. Thankfully we have the book on peace. Our Bible is our personal source of truths and wisdom that usher us to *Jehovah Shalom*.

It is possible to be at peace *with* God and yet never
have the peace *of* God.

The Word on Peace

You can't trust in your circumstances; you can't trust in the world; you can't trust in your flesh. So what do you do? Where do we find the kind of peace that changes us and the way we respond to the pressures of life? We go to the source of all peace, God's heart. And God's heart expressed in His Word reveals to us how to have God's peace that guards our hearts and minds. Here are some verses to get our hearts peace centered.

> "Peace I leave with you; My peace I give to you; not as the world gives do I give to you. Do not let your heart be troubled, nor let it be fearful." (John 14:27)

> "These things I have spoken to you, so that in Me you may have peace. In the world you have tribulation, but take courage; I have overcome the world." (John 16:33)

> Now may the Lord of peace Himself continually grant you peace in every circumstance. The Lord be with you all! (2 Thessalonians 3:16)

The references to peace recorded by the Holy Spirit for our benefit were spoken at times when God's people were under great distress and difficulty. God did not promise that all the difficulties would be taken away; instead, He told us that in Him we have peace because He has overcome the world. It is possible to be at peace *with* God and yet never have the peace *of* God. God's peace comes in two installments. The first is not at all dependent on what we do, and the second is entirely dependent upon us.

1. God made peace with us through Jesus. We didn't earn that—we didn't create all the right circumstances in order to receive that peace. It is

all God. "Therefore, having been justified by faith, we have peace with God through our Lord Jesus Christ" (Romans 5:1). When we receive Him and the power of His blood to justify us by faith, peace is accomplished on our behalf. The peace treaty was signed in His blood and can never be broken.

2. Our responsibility is to be obedient and follow God's instructions so that we experience His whole peace. Look closely at Philippians 4:6-7:

> Be anxious for nothing, but in everything by prayer and supplication with thanksgiving let your requests be made known to God. And the peace of God, which surpasses all comprehension, will guard your hearts and your minds in Christ Jesus.

It is easy to gloss over these verses and miss a specific detail in God's guidance. But it's right there in God's Word: we are not to be anxious. We don't have permission to get stirred up. So without realizing it, we often disobey God.

What is it right now that's making you anxious? It is serious. It's deep. It's difficult. It's hard. I don't for one second want to minimize your troubles or mine by saying, "Just let go of them, it's easy." Our problems and fears are real and tough and sometimes even crippling. All the more reason why we cannot let our circumstances control us.

I have recently had to remind myself that God told me—He didn't suggest—not to be anxious, but instead, to pray. I don't need to call my friend; I don't need to call my daughters; I don't need to go online and get everyone's opinion; I don't need to talk, talk, talk the problem out. I need to pray first. Yes, I can share what I am going through with others, but my first action should be to take my circumstance straight to God. I am to make my requests known with thanksgiving and believing by faith that there is an answer, there is a solution, there is a way, there is hope, and there is strength.

Whatever you and I need for the battles we face has been provided. And the peace of God is ours when we follow the second part of this passage from Philippians:

> Finally, brethren, whatever is true, whatever is honorable, whatever is right, whatever is pure, whatever is lovely, whatever is of good repute, if there is any excellence and if anything worthy of praise, dwell on these things. The things you have learned and received and heard and seen in me, practice these things, and the God of peace will be with you. (Philippians 4:8-9)

So we've been told what not to do: be anxious. And now we are instructed what we *are* to do, and that is to let our minds "dwell on these things." Not skim. Not read and then ignore or save for later when we are less burdened. We are to dwell on those things that God considers praiseworthy. After we spend time thinking on them, then we are to put those behaviors into action as we "practice these things." And the God of peace, *Jehovah Shalom,* will be with us.

God's Peace in All Circumstances

Do you believe peace can belong to you? You have a God named *Jehovah Shalom* whom you can go to, but you have to choose how you respond to what life presents and to what the enemy places in your path. Each time you encounter a person or experience that challenges your peace, ask yourself if you are dwelling on the problem or on God's peace. I know what it is like to be right in the center of a hardship and realize that my focus is far from God's peace. I'm dwelling on the sadness; I'm dwelling on the difficulty; I'm dwelling on the grief; I'm dwelling on the questions, the doubts, the fears; I'm dwelling on my sleeplessness; I'm dwelling on what this or that person's saying.

When that cycle starts, I have already gone against God's instruction for me. I'm far along a path that does not lead to His peace. But when I stop and dwell on the Word of God, everything changes. I'm going to choose to dwell on what is true; I'm going to choose to dwell on what's honorable. I'm going to trust His provision. I'm going to believe what is pure, and I'm going to choose to believe that He can reign and rule and overrule in the ugliness and the mess. In that belief, we can then practice these things. They are not natural or what our flesh will automatically do. We have to train and practice. The peace of God is hard fought. It doesn't come easily. In Colossians, Paul said, "Let the peace of Christ rule in your hearts" (3:15). If the peace of Christ is going to rule your heart, you're going to have to get out of His way and put your problems to the side. You'll have to elevate Him as the ruler over your heart, and when you do that, His peace will come in.

God's peace is available when the winds of adversity are raging against your life. He spoke to the storm when His disciples thought for sure they would sink. He said, "Peace be with you." Those words were for the disciples, and they are for you today. Maybe you're sure that you are going to sink. The winds of adversity and the storms are beating you down. But you're going to have to choose to believe that He can come in the midst of the storm. He might not change the storm. Paul's ship broke all to pieces, but every man arrived on shore alive. If you will look to the One who controls the storm, He will be with you.

Jesus' disciples were terrified after He was crucified. They didn't know if they'd been following a lie or living a dream, so they locked themselves away. They were scared because they were hunted and hated, and they weren't sure what had happened and what was going to happen. They were dwelling on the doubts and on their own insecurities as well as the potential dangers. They were not dwelling on the promises of the Lord.

When Jesus appeared to them, he immediately spoke of peace. "When the doors were shut where the disciples were, for fear of the

Jews, Jesus came and stood in their midst and said to them, 'Peace *be* with you'" (John 20:19).

Maybe you're terrified, or you're very unsure of yourself right now. Jesus can show up when you think there's no possible way, and He can speak peace into your situation. In what part of your life are you trembling, hiding, and dwelling on doubt? Think of your Savior speaking peace over you. He is there with you right now. *Jehovah Shalom* longs for us to experience His presence.

God Meets Us in Our Fear

We first meet *Jehovah Shalom* in a story about Gideon. The encounter is recorded in Judges. I love to study how God shows up in people's lives, so I couldn't resist an opportunity to look more closely at Gideon. To set the scene, Israel had made it into the Promised Land. We've talked about Joshua, the battles, and all that it took for the Israelites to get that far. But after God brought them through so much, they were not obedient. And as a result, they were not enjoying the blessings or the benefits of faithfulness. Times were difficult. The people were being ravaged by the Midianites, who were stealing their harvests and trampling and destroying their land and livestock. These enemies taunted, haunted, and harassed the Israelites. As the suffering continued, the Israelites cried out to God and He sent a prophet. Now, they would have preferred that He had sent a deliverer. Wouldn't that be your first choice? When we're suffering we want someone to lift us up and get us out of the difficult circumstances. But God sent a prophet. He sent His truth and His word through a man who basically said, "You people are reaping what you've sown." That isn't exactly a message of comfort, is it? However, the prophet reminds us that God's blessing and our obedience go hand in hand. Obedience does not mean we will have a carefree life, but it will result in a life that does not reap unnecessary, ungodly consequences for us and those who follow us.

Gideon was caught up in the trials that were caused by the sins of the people who went before him. He was so afraid of the Midianites that he found ways to hide from his enemies while he harvested his wheat. The typical way to harvest wheat was to do it in an open field on a hill so that the chaff separated from the kernels and was carried away by the breeze, allowing more seed to be planted. But Gideon was not on a hill—he was in a winepress below. He was so desperate to self-protect and keep his wheat that he hid and covered up his supplies. Who can blame him for trying to protect what was his and for being afraid of the enemy? Yet this couldn't have been a life of peace—always hiding, covering, being on watch, and worrying that others might take away what he felt he needed to survive.

Do you recognize this behavior at all? Have you ever gone into emotional hiding to self-protect? Maybe you've even found yourself driven into depression as you go to extremes to keep the provision that you believe you need. God saw this behavior in Gideon, and so He appeared to him as an angel. The angel was Jesus Himself, and the first thing He said was, "God is with you, mighty valiant warrior."

This scene makes me laugh a little. Poor Gideon probably looked around and wondered who the angel could possibly be addressing as a valiant warrior. He was, after all, hiding in a cave, hovered over his wheat, scared out of his wits that someone might find him. In his fear, he doubted the validity of the angel and challenged him. "If You are God, why have these things happened to us? Where were You when we needed You, and now what are we going to do?"

What would you do? Or I should say, what have you done when God's presence was made known in your life when you were hovering over your family and your children, trying to keep it all together?

God reminds you that He is with you. God beholds you as a valiant warrior because God sees things in you that you can't possibly see in yourself. Do you trust His view of you? His belief in you? Or have you responded like Gideon with confusion and by playing 20 questions with God? I've responded that way. There have definitely been times when I have cried out questions to God. *If You're God, why did this happen? Why did You allow such a thing? Why did You allow these circumstances in my life? Why did You not give me the version of life I longed for, expected, and prayed for? Why is my plan messed up? Where have You been, God?*

God's response to Gideon was direct. "The LORD looked at him and said, 'Go in this your strength and deliver Israel from the hand of Midian. Have I not sent you?'" (Judges 6:14). So God told the man who was clearly hiding from Midian to go and deliver his people *from* Midian.

What?!

And that's exactly how Gideon responded.

> God will not send you out to stand against an enemy without having your front, your back, and your side. He's got you.

Peace Is Found in God's Strength

Gideon was still caught up in his own flaws and weaknesses. He could not see past his insecurities to God's strength and His offer of might. Gideon said to Him, "O Lord, how shall I deliver Israel? Behold, my family is the least in Manasseh, and I am the youngest in my father's house" (Judges 6:15). See that? Gideon rattled off reasons why he was not a good choice. He had a bad self-image, but then again maybe it was perfect, because God specializes in using people who think that they have absolutely nothing to offer. But God didn't accept those excuses. He promised to be with Gideon.

God's strength is made known in our weakness. "But the Lord said to him, 'Surely I will be with you, and you shall defeat Midian as one man'" (Judges 6:16).

This is the only thing you ever need to know, and God is saying it to you: you are not alone. God will not send you out to stand against an enemy without having your front, your back, and your side. He's got you.

Gideon said, "Well if this is so, then give me…" and he began listing off his requirements and tests of the Lord to convince Him that he really could do this huge thing being asked of him. Of course, God was not asking it of him alone. He was asking Gideon to join *with* Him and to move forward as a warrior in God's strength.

This passage really is remarkable when you think about it. Gideon was bargaining, arguing, and trying to barter back and forth with God. With God! It seems so outrageous. And yet, don't we do the same when God asks us to do something we don't feel capable of or prepared for? We start to question God's ability, not just our own.

In your circumstance right now, the one in which you need victory and peace, God knows the way that you need to take. You can't go the wrong way if you listen to, look to, follow, and obey Him. Gideon said, "Alright, but don't go anywhere, wait. Wait right here. I'm going to get my offering." And so began an entire series of delay tactics on Gideon's part. God was good, gracious, loving, and patient. But when I read this passage, I am done with Gideon. I think, *Lord, just wash Your hands of him. Maybe he isn't worthy of Your trust!* But my thoughts go there because I have forgotten how many times I have said, "Wait Lord, wait. Let me do one more thing." This is so humbling.

Gideon went to get his animal and his unleavened bread, and he set it before the angel of the Lord. The angel touched it with the staff and consumed it with fire. This offering cost Gideon a lot personally. He lived in lack. He and his family likely watched out for every little thing they had, especially livestock and food provisions. That sacrifice softens my heart toward this angst-filled man who was too scared to live and then was willing to act in faith. When we are overwhelmed by our fear, let us remember to act with enough faith to make a move. Even just enough to say, "I'll come out of the cave. I'll come out of the pit. I'll take a chance to make one step of faith toward *Jehovah Shalom*." As He did with Gideon, God will honor it.

When the angel revealed himself and departed, Gideon's eyes were opened in revelation. He then understood that he'd been face to face with God Himself. And he knew that the Word said from the laws of Moses that no man could see God and live. He became terribly afraid, but God said back to him, "Peace to you, do not fear; you shall not die" (Judges 6:23). Do you know what relief, what utter humility must have overcome Gideon when he realized he deserved to die but God had let him live? Instead of killing Gideon, instead of raging against him for his doubt and fear and lists of tests for the Lord, God extended peace. Again, peace.

This is what God wants us to understand in our heart at that moment of revelation: "I deserve to die, but He's let me live, and He's given me the opportunity to go and to serve." At this moment in the story, "Gideon built an altar there to the LORD and named it The LORD is Peace" (Judges 6:24). *Jehovah Shalom* was introduced via a fallible, worried, scared, hiding man who was called to be a warrior and serve God.

> God's peace will raise you up out of your pit of worry and release you from your cave of fear.

God has put a call on your life. He wants you to have His peace, no matter what the circumstances are in your life. Let me ask you, have you had that moment of revelation? Have you maybe had it fresh and new?

I will share with you an embarrassing story about myself. Once, soon after the holiday season, I returned home after a trip and was immediately overwhelmed when I walked through our front door. Decorations lingered, laundry was stacked up, mail was piled on the counter, and there was wreckage in every corner. I didn't know where to start, and I became frenzied and scattered. I would run to the laundry room and pitch something there, and then I'd run back to the kitchen sink and try to clean up there, and then I'd scan other rooms and think, *I need to get those in boxes. No, I need to sort that pile. Wait, I should probably clear the floor first.* The thoughts poured through my mind, but I couldn't grasp on to anything and commit to a next step. Later that night, I told my husband that if there had been a surveillance camera in our kitchen, the images of me would've looked like a chicken with its head cut off. I had to have looked more than a little insane running here and there. I was shuffling things to and from the kitchen island for the umpteenth time when I thought, *Oh my gosh, I'm about to have a breakdown. Why am I so upset and unsettled?* All of a sudden I cried out, "Oh Lord, I'm so sorry. I'm just trying to self-protect and get everything squared away. While I'm scrambling to organize my way to peace, I've totally dismissed You in this picture. The fact that You, *Jehovah Shalom*, would enter into my mess and create order, calm, and peace humbles me."

I went over to the counter and did the only thing I knew to do—I picked up my Bible, my journal, and a pen. And when I sat down with these objects, I realized I had chosen what was most valuable and most precious and had given it priority. Right there in the rubble and the mess, I made an altar. With a shaky voice and a heart eager for peace, I said, "God, You can create order out my disorder and give me peace."

This may sound like a silly example of being deluged by external things. But at the time I was completely overwhelmed until Jesus came and spoke His peace. There are still so many more internal things, such as sadness, loss, emptiness, and difficult or tender memories, and the pain can wash over us for a long time. Regrets can haunt us with the "could've, should've, and would've" taunts. Many things can threaten to steal our peace. But when we pause and experience the presence of *Jehovah Shalom,* He is there and His peace is abundant.

Encountering Jehovah Shalom

Trusting Jehovah Shalom

1. View a current obstacle or fear as the enemy's attack on your spiritual peace. Now turn to *Jehovah Shalom* in prayer. Consider if you have experienced the two installments of God's peace. First, do you accept and believe that God has made peace with you through Christ? And second, are you obedient and following God's Word so that you walk and live in peace? Start training in the ways of God's peace so that your first instinct will be to trust Him in every circumstance.

2. Think of Gideon's responses to *Jehovah Shalom*. When have you distrusted God's strength to replace your own? When have you finally believed His voice and taken steps forward in faith? What happened?

Remembering the Benefits of Jehovah Shalom

1. When you are empowered by *Jehovah Shalom*, you can do anything He calls you to do. Draw closer to His heart and to His Word so that your first thoughts during a time of stress are of His peace that surpasses all understanding. What is He asking you to move toward right now in His peace and strength?

2. Are you dwelling on your fear or a potential threat to your peace? Shift your thoughts to dwell on that which is true, honorable, right, pure, lovely, of good repute, excellent, and worthy of praise. When you dwell on eternal things, you will

feel the peace on an emotional, physical, and spiritual level. This week, each time fear rises, turn your thoughts to these things and believe the benefit of trusting *Jehovah Shalom*. The God of peace will be with you, right there in the midst of your greatest fear.

Blessing Jehovah Shalom

1. God, as our Peace, is with us in our darkest places. He is with us when we are scared and scattered. Have you had a day when you were rushing from task to task and you could not get calm? Or maybe your need for peace is felt on a spiritual level, and you are lost in a time of doubting God or His love for you. Act with faith. Bless *Jehovah Shalom* by building an altar to Him in the midst of your craziness, in the middle of a time of panic. His presence is with you. Can you feel it? You bless Him when you set aside your excuses, regrets, and claims of being unworthy. You bless Him when you trust His strength over your own and you step forward in faith to serve, to be a valiant warrior.

2. What gnaws at your peace lately? What ways have you tried to find peace other than going to *Jehovah Shalom*? List these empty sources and then surrender them to Him. Bless Him by being singular in your faithfulness. Stand on Him as the only source of peace you need for what brings you fear or frenzy now and what could undermine your peace in the future.

Praying to Jehovah Shalom

Jehovah Shalom, *thank You that You are the Prince of Peace. I worship and exalt You as the Lord over all. I pray that Your Spirit reveals to me what I am trying to self-protect from and what I am hovering over, trying to save in my limited human power. Help me to leave behind the way of excuses and regrets. I want to have open eyes and a revelation of knowledge and understanding of Your truth and peace. Thank You for Your patience and Your lovingkindness. I ask that You go before me now and prepare me so that wherever I go and whatever I do, no matter what the circumstances are, I will choose to practice those things that are of eternal value. You breathe peace into my life! Thank You for Your power. In Jesus' name. Amen.*

7

Follow the Lead of *Jehovah Roi*

God Is Your Shepherd

Have you found yourself in a spiritual valley lately? Or maybe you've been taking labored steps up an emotional mountainside. When our journey takes us to places of worry and fear; when we become lost in the world and feel unseen and unloved; or when we face a battle and are defenseless, we know the need for our Shepherd, *Jehovah Roi.*

Throughout his life, David had times of great blessing and tremendous loss. He knew victory and defeats personally and on the battlefront, but through it all, he had a special hope and trust in the Lord as his Shepherd. He understood the preciousness of this relationship because he didn't start as a king—he started his life of faith as a young shepherd boy. This role, and later, this understanding of God as Shepherd, as *Jehovah Roi,* shaped David's loving relationship with the Lord. The peace he found in *Jehovah Roi* led him to say, "The Lord is my shepherd, I shall not want. He makes me lie down in green pastures; He leads me beside quiet waters. He restores my soul; He guides me in the paths of righteousness for His name's sake" (Psalm 23:1-3).

You and I probably have not tended too many sheep or actually been herded through a meadow by a staff and rod, but the illustration of the relationship between a shepherd and his sheep can be the most vivid and peace giving. Scripture overflows with these illustrations. In Genesis we are told that Abel was a keeper of sheep. So from the very beginning, God has used sheep and shepherds to give us personal pictures of an important relationship. Abraham, Isaac, and Jacob were patriarchs who learned about God and from God through their experiences as shepherds. When Joseph's people went down to Egypt, God made them a great nation. He separated them from the Egyptians; He put them aside in the land of Goshen. Out of the shepherd's fields, He raised up a people that was separate and set apart and sanctified for His use and His purpose.

The people of Old Testament times didn't have a Bible and didn't have the Holy Spirit, but they did have a living example of God's care and guidance. In the middle of their strife and in times of blessing, they could understand that the relationship between the Shepherd and His fallible, fragile sheep was dear. And you and me—we are those sheep!

The Thing About Sheep

Learning about sheep can help us learn about our relationship with the Shepherd. I did some research about them and discovered that they are by nature timid, fearful, and easily panicked. They're gullible and innocent. They are prone to wander. They are vulnerable to mob psychology, which means they follow where the herd goes and pay no attention to the dangers ahead. Their only defense if there is trouble is to run away, so they're easily killed off by their enemies.

Sheep are stubborn and competitive for dominance. They stay on the move in search of fresh water and fresh pasture. But they don't have discernment, so they will drink contaminated water and food that can hurt them, even kill them. A fascinating and rather visually amusing aspect of sheep is that they are easily cast, which means they easily get flipped over onto their backs and can't get back up. Poor sheep. They don't like to be sheared, and they don't like to be cleaned up. They frequently are looking for a place to rest. They're creatures of habit, and they get into a rut, preferring a pattern for grazing. They are the neediest of any livestock. They are lost without their shepherd.

I will be completely honest. This describes me! My list of flaws and vulnerabilities are right there in black and white. There is no question about it. Timid, fearful, and easily panicked. Does this describe you? If you take your eyes off of Jesus, do you feel like the first and the only thing you want to do is turn and run?

What about being easily cast? Can you relate to flailing about, unable to get right side up? It's embarrassing to confess, but that's so me. There are circumstances that throw me for a loop and make me want to quit. Life can be too hard, too heavy. When life and hope are upside down, I admit that I can remain in that flail for a long time: unsure of what to do next, uncertain that I want to get back on my feet, and unaware of a way to change the course of my path.

But wait—there is hope for these creatures and for us! Why? Because sheep are also easily influenced by a leader. They are stubborn and lack common sense, yet their nature seeks a shepherd's call and leading. They have to have a shepherd, and the shepherd is the most influential and effective influence that a sheep will ever have. David knew this influence and this care when he wrote, "Surely goodness and lovingkindness will follow me all the days of my life, and I will dwell in the house of the LORD forever" (Psalm 23:6).

I want to tell you from my own experience that the most effective and the most influential shepherd that I know is God the Shepherd. If this sheep could just learn to be totally and fully dependent on my Good Shepherd, I would not stray, I would not be alone, and I would discover the gift of being led safely by *Jehovah Roi* who speaks to me so I can understand Him. He gives me His Word so I can understand Him and my nature as a sheep.

Our dear *Jehovah Roi* gives each of us His promises through His Word. And He calls our name because He knows us and we know to listen for and trust His voice. "I am the good shepherd, and I know My own and My own know Me, even as the Father knows Me and I know the Father; and I lay down My life for the sheep" (John 10:14-15).

When We Stray

Do you feel like you are part of the flock but are dangerously close to falling away? You know it happens. Being a stray is never what we aspire to. Have you ever seen a stray dog running down the street alone? You feel so bad for it; you want to help it find a place to go, because strays so often wander into precarious and dangerous places. Places of compromise.

Recently I was dangerously close to straying. You might find that surprising and wonder how that could happen. Believe me, it can happen quickly and when we're unaware. I wasn't expecting it, but one day I felt myself slipping over the edge. Prone to wander. Oh, I wasn't going to go do anything crazy, but I could tell that it would not take much for me to fall into a pit. In my discouragement, I thought, *I don't know if the Lord's enough. Unlike David, I do want. My need is great and I am lost.* In that moment, I wasn't looking at my Good Shepherd. I was forgetting that He had promised to supply every need. You could say that I was cast. The flailing had started, and the fear was coursing through me.

Then, by His Holy Spirit, He came to me. That is what He does. He tenderly and gently begins to draw you back into the fold, and He ministers to you. He corrects you. He takes the rod, He takes the staff, and He says, "Get your eyes on Me. You will see My compassion. You don't need to stray, to fall from the path, or to scoot under the fence. Get back close to Me. I will take you back into the fold and lead you."

We Are All Vulnerable

I imagine that you know what it feels like to get over the edge, to feel like you just might slip over or fall in, but the Good Shepherd will come and pick you up and carry you. No matter what and no matter why you are facing the edge. We all have our vulnerabilities.

There isn't a station or season in life that will protect us from becoming lost. Only the Shepherd protects. Some face a life situation that discourages them because it is so different from what they had imagined for themselves. Singles who long to be in marriage. Divorced women who walked down the aisle in a white dress with dreams of sharing their forever with a husband. A widow who mourns the loss of her husband. The mom who is struggling to stay sane and upright in the face of seemingly endless demands. Every person has times of vulnerability when they think it will be simpler, more desirable, or safer to separate from the flock and to find their own way. Sometimes our community, even one that loves us, reminds us of our aloneness, our losses, and our fears. We start to protect our vulnerable hearts in the way sheep are likely to respond to any danger—we run away. When we are scared, that solution feels like our only defense.

When we're lost, confused, disappointed, and disillusioned, *Jehovah Roi* will not say, "Get lost. Stay out. Three strikes and you're done."

But the sweet thing, the precious thing is to remember that Jesus will go and get a stray. He will leave the group to go after one. And if I asked you to declare that you have been the one that He's come after, I imagine that you could say, "I know what it is to stray and be far away. I have felt isolated, left out, and alone. In my pain I have chosen to be separated from others because I was too stubborn or too scared to go back to where I knew I needed to be."

Where else would you go? May I ask, where have you been? Did you find a place where your needs were fully met, where the supply was endless, and where there was always the food that you needed for your soul besides Jesus? No. You found a place that set you apart from Him! And when you are there, you're not guarded. You are not safe anywhere else but in the sheepfold.

If this is you right this very moment, would you go back? Listen for *Jehovah Roi*.

He said He wants you to return to the Shepherd and the Guardian of your soul. And even in our vulnerable state of being, we are accepted. We are never rejected. God does not cast us out. When we're lost, confused, disappointed, and disillusioned, *Jehovah Roi* will not say, "Get lost. Stay out. Three strikes and you're done." No, He says, "Return. Return to Me."

If you are far away from the Shepherd's watch today, return to the Guardian of your soul. The one who can meet any need. The one who can set any captive spirit free. The only one who can heal the diseased and take that broken or stubborn heart and change it and make it new.

Our Deep Need for a Shepherd

"The Lord is my shepherd, I shall not want" (Psalm 23:1) can be thought of as: My Shepherd is the Lord, so I want nothing. Is this statement true for you? My Shepherd is the Lord. Really think about this and your life right now. Is *Jehovah Roi* the one you are listening to and following? Is it His rod and staff that guide you back to safety?

Consider whether the way you live your life reflects this psalm from David. Be sure you don't have a substitution in place. God doesn't say your husband is the Good Shepherd. He doesn't say your friend or pastor or teacher is the Good Shepherd. When you recognize that the Lord is your Good Shepherd, you will say, "I want nothing else. He is my full supply. He has all that I need; He is *the* source." And it's amazing to discover that you not only have all that you need but you have all that you want, because your wants begin to change. They too begin to follow the loving Shepherd and His best for you.

What do I want? I want peace. He says, "Oh, I'm peace. I'm *Jehovah Shalom*." You say, "I want order, joy, wisdom, strength, courage, and I want all that God has for me. I want forgiveness and love. I want to be able to minister and to give and to tend to others. I want the Holy Spirit." Jesus is the source of and the way to all these good things. In your time of want, the Shepherd appears.

Our Shepherd Appears

Scripture is full of so many wonderful moments. A scene so dear to me, especially in light of our journey right now, is when the Good Shepherd showed up to the shepherds. He *chose* shepherds when it was time to share His message for all people. The Christ child was to be born into a world of lost sheep. And while the shepherds were watching over their flocks by night, the angel came and said, "I've got good tidings and great joy and good news, and it's for all people" (Luke 2:10, paraphrase).

In return, in that full circle beauty of God's Word and God's unfolding message, it was the shepherds who went to see Him first. He came. When He came, He experienced the desperation and the depravation of people and of mankind. The needs, the foolishness, the stubbornness. If you go back and read through the gospel, take in the stories of the state of mankind when Jesus came. The needy people were following after Him. They were lost and in His presence, they were found. The state of mankind hasn't really changed at all!

How thankful we are that we have the time He walked on earth chronicled. We know that during this time He saw the needs and the needy people. He saw the dire circumstances and the darkened hearts, and His heart ached because His sheep were misled. His precious sheep had followed false shepherds. He had compassion rather than anger because He also saw that the people had not been met in their place of need. They had been ignored and overlooked, and they began to wander. They were just sheep, and so they followed whomever was in front of them. And what was in front of them at that time were religion and the law and a mindset of keeping the rules and following the regulations. Their focus was who was clean and who was unclean. They created a system of distance and separation rather than one that gathered together the flock of God. Every town was filled with people who walked by the local outcast and set apart the town lepers—they refused to touch or help the disabled outsiders. Anyone who did not fit the picture of holy and perfect and righteous was avoided and ignored. Just like today, nobody really wanted to see the frailty of vulnerability and need.

But Jesus saw it. He saw *them*. The Shepherd appeared, and He began to go and reach and touch those who had been cast aside. He could hear the bleating, the cries of those who were lost and dying. When there is no shepherd and there is no master, the results are deadly, and the cost is life. How the sounds of pain and death must break the Shepherd's heart.

He said, "The thief comes only to steal and kill and destroy; I came that they may have life, and have it abundantly" (John 10:10). Christ came so that we might have life. Even now, people are crying for life, hope, and help. People are desperate; people are doing crazy things. Just watch television one night. Just read the newspaper. Just read the news that scrolls alongside your online searches.

The sheep are crying—there's bleating everywhere, maybe even in your own home.

When you know God as *Jehovah Roi,* there are two ways to look at everything. You are a sheep; and if you are a believer, you are also called to be a shepherd. When you have been rescued from death and carried home in the loving arms of the Shepherd, you are compelled to help others back to the fold and to the safe haven of a compassionate Lord's care.

The Compelling Compassion of *Jehovah Roi*

In Mark there is a description of Jesus that I turned over and over in my mind and heart during this journey with *Jehovah Roi* because it says so much about the Lord we serve. "When Jesus went ashore, He saw a large crowd, and He felt compassion for them because they were like sheep without a shepherd; and He began to teach them many things" (Mark 6:34). As soon as He saw the crowd, He had compassion. He looked with compassion on this group of needy, wanting, hurting people. I thought a lot about that because this response is exceptional. This is a pure illustration of the Shepherd's love in action. Another translation states that Jesus was "moved with compassion" (NKJV). Only our sweet Lord could have such mercy for such a motley crew of lost sheep.

When Jesus looks, He looks with compassion. His heart perceives the things that are in people's hearts, and He witnesses what goes on in their lives with tenderness. He doesn't just look with sympathy. Sympathy and compassion are two different things. Compassion compels you to do something. The people awaiting Jesus on the shore were hungry. They were so hungry for hope and direction. They were hungry to be cared for. And Jesus was compelled to save, lead, heal, and care for those He encountered.

Are you hungry for hope? Nothing but the Lord will satisfy that gnawing in the deepest, innermost part of your being. The doctor's reports won't satisfy, the teacher's praise won't satisfy, the job market won't satisfy, your financial bottom line just won't satisfy. I don't know what your situation is, but He knows, and He looks with compassion and is compelled by it. When Jesus encountered this hunger for hope among the people that day, He totally changed His plans. He had been planning to go off to a quiet place. He was longing to be away from the crowds so He could be with His disciples, teach them, train them, and be blessed by them. He also wanted to prepare them for the imminent time when He would no longer walk beside them.

However, when He saw the people, He rearranged His whole schedule. He was totally inconvenienced. This greatly convicts me. How about you? Are you willing to be inconvenienced? Are you ministering to others, shepherding those God entrusts to you, and looking with compassion, not just sympathy? Rather than saying, "She's got it rough, and I am so sad," think about how you can come alongside her to pray and teach. Share Jesus as the answer and the source of all any of us ever needs, because He is the Good Shepherd. And He can be trusted with everything because He gave nothing less than His life. Jesus laid down His life for the sheep.

Your needs and my needs move Him to compassion. That touches my heart. He wants to be our Shepherd, and He wants to be our Master. He wants to teach us about Himself, and He wants to teach you to be a good shepherd so you can point others to Him. One way we become a shepherd who draws people to Christ is to have and show compassion. Are you willing to pray, "Lord, open my eyes, move me with compassion"?

Following Our Shepherd's Lead

Moses shepherded the most obstinate, cranky people through the wilderness for 40 long and difficult years. When he was nearing the end of his life, he asked God, "May the Lord, the God of the spirits of all flesh, appoint a man over the congregation, who will go out and come in before them, and who will lead them out and bring them in, so that the congregation of the Lord will not be like sheep which have no shepherd" (Numbers 27:16-17). Moses wanted to be sure that the people he loved were taken care of by a new leader. He went to God on behalf of his flock.

At the heart of this request is a prayer that you can make on behalf of the people that you love and care for and about. Consider going to God and asking that He would raise up someone, a man or a woman, who would lead them out and lead them in and take them to the Good Shepherd. Would you be willing to be a shepherd in somebody else's life? You could be the person somebody else is praying for to lead them out and lead them in.

You're a sheep in the large flock of the body of Christ, and you are also a shepherd of whomever the Lord has put under your sphere of influence. Consider if you are shepherding the people that God is bringing into your sphere of influence. Are you caring, loving, corrective, and invested in their well-being? Do you have *Jehovah Roi's* compassion toward these people?

My husband, Frank, is one of the most compassionate people I have ever known, and he didn't start that way. Not that he wasn't nice, but God has done work on him over the years. God has honed his heart to become compassionate like that of our Shepherd.

One evening when Frank and I were at a pizza place, a pleasant, well-spoken man in his early 40s waited on us. After the waiter took our order, Frank looked up at me and said, "I wonder what that man's story is." He knew that there was a reason, some reason, why this man was working in a pizza place in this season of his life. I looked at him and said, "I don't know. What are you going to do?"

His response was that of a man with the Shepherd's heart. "I'm just going to pray for him. I'm going to let him know." So before we left, Frank took time to encourage our waiter. He thanked him for doing a good job and having a servant's attitude. He blessed him. He poured out compassion. He paid attention and saw someone who needed a word of encouragement, and he acted out of compassion.

When God asks us to be a shepherd in someone's life, He calls us to care, to see past the surface, and to be touched by the things that other people struggle with. Who or what moves you to compassion? If busyness or anxiety tend to cloud your awareness, ask the Lord each day to open your eyes and to show you those around you who need a moment with a shepherd and who need a lifetime with *Jehovah Roi*.

Maybe you have someone in your life who has strayed away from the flock and you are wondering if they are too far away to reach. Nobody is too far away for the Lord to embrace. Nobody is too insignificant; nobody is too impossible. Would you pray? Pray for the lost sheep. There are people everywhere whose hearts are heavy because they have lost sheep that are part of their fold, part of their sphere of influence. The person might not be lost or far away— they might be right in your own house, but they are far away from the Lord! They're disconnected from the body of Christ, they're not part of the flock, they're not following the leader, and they have no master. It is likely that the world is their master or their work is their master or their desire for approval has become their master.

If you are worried about having the ability to be a shepherd, you will find comfort in Hebrews: "Now the God of peace, who brought up from the dead the great Shepherd of the sheep through the blood of the eternal covenant, even Jesus our Lord, equip you in every good thing to do His will, working in us that which is pleasing in His sight, through Jesus Christ" (Hebrews 13:20-21). God will give you the strength to do His will, so ask Him to give you a shepherd's heart for the lost sheep. Ask to have a shepherd's heart for your family, neighbors, friends, and the people God is bringing into your circle. Be willing to invest in your flock.

Jesus walked with His flock. He sat with them. He pulled water up from the well for them. He lifted them up off a mat. He reached through the messiness of their humanity so that He could show them love and grace. Our dear *Jehovah Roi* entered into the lives of the people that He came to save. And today, I truly believe, He's asking you and me to be willing to enter into the lives of other people. They might not be beautiful, they might not be easy, and they might be outcasts. They might even be people who have caused you pain in the past. But if you are called to behold them as your flock, God will give you the love and strength to care for them.

Go after someone in prayer, go after them in compassion, and begin to minister to them. Maybe you don't even say a word, but you show them the love of Jesus and the care of Jesus. They may begin to ask you, "Why would you do this? Why do you care?" And then you have an open door to share more about the Good Shepherd.

God's Care All of Our Lives

I don't know what causes your weariness right now, but I do know that *Jehovah Roi* will gather His lambs and He will carry them in His bosom to safety, nourishment, and rest. His tenderness is great for those who care for others. Maybe you are a mom who would give anything for a weekend alone just to sleep. Perhaps you're the caregiver of your mother or your father and you struggle under the demands of the decisions but also the emotional weight of seeing your strong parent revert to childlike needs. Perhaps there's somebody in your life who is physically or developmentally delayed, requiring a lot of care and attention.

Jehovah Roi calls to each of us in our need and says, "I take you up, young mother. I take you up, caregiver. When you're depleted and drained of everything it takes, I will take you up. I will carry you, and I will give you what you need."

He also says that when we're old and gray, He will not forsake us. I can tell you that with each passing year, this comfort becomes more precious! It is hard to get old. It is scary to worry about the needs we might have in the future, but our thoughts can always return to the certainty of the Shepherd's presence. He's everything for every person. The Holy Spirit of God touches and heals. He fills your cup until it runs over, so that whatever life looks like, you can say, "This is my testimony too. The goodness of the Lord has followed me all the days of my life, the good ones and the not so good ones, and I will dwell in His presence forever and ever. Amen."

He is your Shepherd, and He will never show up without something to feed you. He will never take you to a place that has bitter water. The Good Shepherd always takes you to a place of living water and provides what you need. Are you looking to the Shepherd? Do you hear the voice of *Jehovah Roi* who knows your every need? He goes after His sheep; He uses His crook, and He uses His rod.

Sometimes He simply waits. He says, "Return, return."

Encountering Jehovah Roi

Trusting Jehovah Roi

1. We are the needy sheep who depend on the care and guidance of our Shepherd. Listen for His voice closely this week and all the days to follow. Pray to be emptied of all other wants so that your only need is the guidance of *Jehovah Roi.* Think about where He is leading you in your life right now. Feel God leading you through the obstacles of fear and hesitation and onto a path of faith and security in Him alone.

2. Ask God to show you how to have compassion for those that He has placed in your life today. Pray for those who are difficult for you to connect with or have empathy for. In your quiet time, pray to have a heart like His. When He calls you to serve, lead, or care for another of His sheep, trust that He will give you all that you need to follow through. Does someone specific come to mind?

Remembering the Benefits of Jehovah Roi

1. Have you come to a place of spiritual exhaustion? Your dear *Jehovah Roi* will restore your soul. He will accompany you through the darkness and the difficult terrain of whatever you face in this life season. In your weariness, go to the Shepherd's presence for His care.

2. What sources other than God have you sought in order to fill your want and need? Give those to *Jehovah Roi* and then turn to Him in your need. He has given His life so that you will have life. Remember this by repeating and memorizing this verse. "I am the good shepherd, and I know My own and My

own know Me, even as the Father knows Me and I know the Father; and I lay down My life for the sheep" (John 10:14-15). Be a woman who knows her Shepherd and thinks of Him first when scared or tempted to stray. What leads you to the Shepherd today?

Blessing Jehovah Roi

1. Take time each morning to ask God to fill you with wants and needs that are of Him. Ask for His longings. When you start your days in prayer to seek *Jehovah Roi's* will for your life, you will be amazed at how it impacts your choices, decisions, and your power to follow through. The wants and needs that arise will be those that compel you to act in His will. You will be in line with where the Good Shepherd is guiding you. This obedience will bless Him and His flock.

2. When you see others with the Shepherd's love and compassion, you are closer to becoming like Him. Bless *Jehovah Roi* by becoming a faithful shepherd in the body of Christ. What specific ways is God calling you to lead, love, guide, teach, or mentor? Spend time praying for direction and then take the first steps involved in being a devoted shepherd.

Praying to Jehovah Roi

Jehovah Roi, You are the Good Shepherd. What more could I want? I don't want to ever be tempted to take a long, cool drink anywhere but from the living water. So I thank You and I praise You that You are my Shepherd. You know my name and I know Yours. You've looked with compassion on me and on all of Your sheep. Help me to depend on Your strength. And create in me a heart to lead others back to You.

I think of all the times You have sought me out when I was afraid, alone, and tempted to stay on the edge of the flock. Your faithfulness fills my heart with awe and joy. May I turn my gratitude into a daily desire to follow Your voice with complete trust and follow Your lead by becoming a shepherd in the body of Christ. In Jesus' name I pray. Amen.

8

Wait Patiently with *El Olam*

God Is Everlasting

*W*hat time is it? How much time is left? When do I need to be there?" On any given day, most of us ask these questions at least once. Our days are defined by time, and we are often confined by time. That is our human nature. That isn't God's nature. He is everlasting. Our understanding of time as a limited resource can make it difficult for us to understand or believe God's everlasting nature.

El Olam means "God Everlasting." *Olam* is the Hebrew word for "What endures forever." In Him there is no beginning and there is no end. Olam does not just mean timeless or forever; it means that which has no beginning and no end. Everlasting means He won't wear out or wear down. When we focus on our human frailty and limitations, it is hard to grasp the concept of an existence that is not bound by time and physical limits. For example, how can we begin to understand where God came from? If God didn't have a mother or a father, where did He come from? He always was. He always is. He always will be. That is everlasting.

Our *El Olam* is outside of time because He created time. He marked the days from the very beginning because He is beyond time. Even if this is difficult for us to take in, there is great comfort in this truth about who God is. But first we have to really know it, hear it, and believe this amazing truth about our Lord. "Have you not known? Have you not heard? The everlasting God, the LORD, the Creator of the ends of the earth, neither faints nor is weary. His understanding is unsearchable" (Isaiah 40:28 NKJV).

❖❖❖❖❖

We won't ever fully understand God, but we can
understand His nature.

I want to ask you the same question that Isaiah asked the people of Israel: "Have you not known? Have you not heard?" Our God is, was, and will be the Everlasting God. If you have known about God and attended church since you were little, you might say, "Yes, I've heard. I've heard with my ears." But have you heard with spiritual ears? Have you seen with spiritual eyes the power and reach of the everlasting God in your own life?

Embracing God's Vastness

We can be transformed when we stop giving power to time and we start trusting and honoring the power of the Everlasting God in our daily life. He formed the world and will always be God. He cannot wear down and He cannot wear out. He is the Creator of the ends of the world. Moses' words express this. "Lord, You have been our dwelling place in all generations. Before the mountains were born or You gave birth to the earth and the world, even from everlasting to everlasting, You are God" (Psalm 90:1-2).

Because we know all these things are true, we need to ask ourselves, "Why do we reduce God to what we can understand? Why do we make Him so small?" Why would we do that when He has come and offered Himself? His Word has provided the promise of so much more than our limiting view. His understanding is vast and unsearchable. We won't ever fully understand God, but we can understand His nature. And we will understand it more as we give our life over to Him.

How have you felt your own limitations lately? Is there a particular trouble that has you feeling stuck and unable to see beyond your needs? Do you view your personal circumstances, relationships, and struggles with hopelessness? Where our vision fails, His goes on forever. Where our energy wanes, His burns brightly. Where our steps falter, His path is sure.

In our journey with *El Shaddai*, we talked about God's sufficiency for our times in the waiting room experiences of life. As we try to make sense of the vastness of *El Olam*, my thoughts return to our times of waiting, waiting, and waiting some more. Think about our society's attitude toward waiting. It is common to express, "I hate to wait. I don't want to wait in line. I don't want to wait my turn. I don't want to wait for results. I can't wait." Our impatience limits us.

We toggle between our technological lifelines, trying to take in messages while also skimming the life events of others on social media. Fast, fast, fast. So much information comes at us, and we also leave a trail of information at warp speed. When we step away from the technology to be out and about, we walk at a hurried pace. We say things like, "I gotta go. Can you get that to me now? I'd stay and talk, but I'm already halfway out the door."

Our impatience is not only evident when we are dreading something. It rises up when we are waiting for something good. We say, "I'm so excited! I can't wait!" Think of a child anticipating the gifts of Christmas morning. Their eagerness is nearly painful as they count down the minutes before bedtime and then the seconds before they can open that first gift the next morning. Adults are impatient too.

In fact, I don't doubt that more than a few mothers find waiting for the end of Christmas break to be a bit painful!

I've expressed some silly times of waiting, but I know that during the painful times of enduring, of trying to trust God, the waiting is anything but funny. It is beyond us. That is why we need the perspective and hope of *El Olam*. The key to the power and strength that God gives is to wait upon the Lord.

Do you get flustered when you wait on the Lord? Do you get angry? Do you start to look for answers from any and every source? Or do you finally rest in God and place your hope in Him? I pray that in whatever you are facing right now, you can wait in confidence and in expectation of His care. Don't try to merely pass time. Wait on the Lord with an active and ready hope; wait with keen spiritual eyes and ears, fully trusting that He knows every detail. His understanding of your situation, circumstance, relationship, or challenge is beyond your own. His knowledge is so vast and His ways are unsearchable. That means we need to trust.

While I'm waiting, I can be confident that He knows exactly what I need when I need it. Everlasting God will come. I won't know how it will look when He does, but I do know that He will be faithful.

> Faithful waiting isn't about trying to make time slip away faster. It is about having hopeful expectation.

Expanding Our View of Waiting

The most amazing thing happens in the waiting room: He renews your strength. Renewal is a by-product of waiting. You will not be renewed if you refuse to wait. Our culture leans toward belief that waiting is fruitless time. A necessary evil, but not the space of time when something good happens. But as believers, we can claim an expansive view of waiting. The waiting room is used to prepare and equip us for what's ahead. It's in waiting that renewal and change comes.

El Olam invites us to do what might seem impossible, at least initially. In the waiting room we are to stop looking for relief, stop looking for an answer, and stop looking to be rescued. I know that is counterintuitive. We want to make good use of the time. In fact, it is easy to believe that we are doing the spiritual work we are supposed to do when we try to solve the problem or force a remedy. Isn't that where we put so much energy when we are in the middle of the seemingly endless trial? When a burden threatens to weigh us down indefinitely, of course we want relief. We pray that our hope will come in a tidy solution that removes the unwelcomed problem or discomfort and that this remedy can be our testimony. That is the very limited human perspective of the waiting.

So how do we stop looking for solutions and start looking to *El Olam* to make something new within us during these times? When you are in this kind of experience, and that might even be right now, change your thoughts from, "How will this be taken from me so that I don't have to wait or worry anymore?" to "God wants to do something in me. Maybe the change that I'm so desperately running after is right here in the waiting room."

The renewing and the refreshing happens in His presence. We can wholeheartedly be in the presence of *El Olam* and wait, knowing that there might not be a change in the circumstance, but there most certainly will be a change within *us*.

Does it seem too difficult to change to this perspective? I promise you, there is great hope in this view of troubled times or grief or uncertainty. When you are in a low place that you have never seen before and probably have prayed to avoid, let go of the former way of waiting. Embrace the understanding that God will transform you from the inside out during this time and that it is not a useless, regrettable time of waiting. In fact, it is an active time even if we feel as though we are making zero progress. So much is stirring within our spirit.

I don't know what's happening in your waiting room, but God knows. Like Paul said in 2 Corinthians 4:7-9, "But we have this treasure in earthen vessels, so that the surpassing greatness of the power will be of God and not from ourselves; we are afflicted in every way, but not crushed; perplexed, but not despairing; persecuted, but not forsaken; struck down, but not destroyed."

You are not destroyed and you will not be destroyed. Not in the endless realm of eternity. *El Olam* is with you during your difficulty, even when it feels like it might define you and destroy you. He comes in and transforms your heart so that you too are living with an eternal perspective and are able to walk forward in life with a sense of eternity rather than earthly limits.

Shifting from Limited to Limitless

You might wonder how I can talk so certainly about this, especially when I don't know the pain you are enduring or have endured. I know because I have journeyed through great loss and I have had to set my eyes on *El Olam*. During the first six to eight months after my son died, people would ask me how I was. That question, or rather, the answer to that question, becomes muddled when you start examining what people will think. If I said, "I'm fine," I realized that people might think I wasn't dealing with it or that I was putting on a fake front or the armor of human stubbornness. Then again, if I said something like, "I'm really in a low place and I'm about to fall apart at the seams," they might wonder, "Where's Jesus?"

Have you been through this kind of thought process? It is taxing, confusing, and makes for more weariness than hope because you feel that your faith and circumstances will be judged and defined by what other people think. Of course, *El Olam* is with us right then and is guiding us toward an eternal perspective that goes far beyond what peers say about us and definitely beyond how we judge and define ourselves. Here is how *El Olam* showed up in my pain.

One day I was reading Scripture, and I decided to wait in the presence of the Lord. I wanted to bypass grief. I wanted to bypass pain, and I wanted to get better fast. God said, "No! Come back to the waiting room." It was in the waiting room that He gave me those precious words from Paul to hold on to. I am going to repeat them from my perspective, and I encourage you to do the same for whatever pain you hold right now. "I am hard pressed but I am not crushed. I am persecuted with memories and things I want with every fiber of my being to change, but I am not in despair. I am struck down, but I am not destroyed."

If you still wonder how I said this or if you wonder how you might possibly muster the strength to say this, it is important to reflect on who gave us these words. Paul was in prison. He was misunderstood, beaten, tortured, on the run, never appreciated, never included, never accepted. Yet he said these things. He faced ridiculous persecution, and he literally was in a prison of restriction and restraint. But he knew the God of no limits. He'll come. I'm expecting Him. I'm not sure what time He'll show up, I don't know when the door will open. I don't know if it will be late at night or early in the morning, but this much I know: He will come. Somebody will ask, "But what if He doesn't?" Oh, He will! He told me in His Word that He would never leave nor forsake me. He told us that His understanding is unsearchable. He told me in His Word, "I am here, and I want to renew your strength. I want to lift you up."

God Gives and Restores

God is a giver. The world wants to take, but God wants to give. God gives power to the weak. When you grow weak or weary and become tired physically, emotionally, and spiritually, He increases your strength. As we age, people tell us that our usefulness is in question or that our time of productivity may be coming to a close. If someone feels weak in any way or "less than" capable, they desperately try to cover up their weakness and make sure that the world understands they haven't lost their strength. But God encourages us by reminding us that even young people faint and grow weary. Even young people fall. "Though youths grow weary and tired, and vigorous young men stumble badly, yet those who wait for the LORD will gain new strength; they will mount up with wings like eagles, they will run and not get tired, they will walk and not become weary" (Isaiah 40:30-31).

Everlasting God is the solution. He is the source of our renewal and restoration when we think we will have to give up. The great gift we are given through *El Olam* is that we don't have to cover up our weakness; we don't have to try to make up for our insecurities and our inabilities. We don't have to try to negate our weariness or exhaustion with activity. When we look at ourselves and look around us and get depressed because there is no source that will save us from our deep lack, God says, "Do not worry. Do not be preoccupied with your weakness. I will provide what you cannot provide for yourself. I can provide what the world can't."

Just keep looking up. Trust Him. He's coming. You have the prayers of the saints and people standing with you, and they remind you that God will show up. God will be what you need Him to be. God's a healer and a restorer. He is your peace. Wait in His presence, and wait in His Word.

Is there something in your life right now that seems to be getting beyond your control? You just can't keep your arms around it any longer. *El Olam* is there with you. The circumstances may never change, but you begin to change in that waiting room. You will be able to say, "I know He's coming because I know whom I have believed, and I am persuaded. He is able to keep that which I have committed to Him. He's coming. He's *El Olam*, Everlasting God. Nothing gets by Him."

You may be down for a little while, but God will raise you up with wings like eagles. And then *El Olam* will set your feet back on the ground, because God's will and God's work in the believer's life is for us to be renewed. Not just so that we feel better, but so that we can go forward and serve Him and glorify His name.

How might you be called to serve out of strength gained by the very circumstance you prayed to have removed?

Saved to Serve

When God saves us, we honor Him with our service and with a spirit that does not quit, withdraw, or hide from living again. Abraham did this when he planted a shade tree in the desert. This tree was a declaration that the Everlasting God would accomplish His Word. God had given Abraham a promise. God told Abraham he would have descendants, that there would be as many as the stars in the sky and the sands on the seashore. He had one little boy. So when he planted a tree, he made a declaration. He told the world around him, "I'm going to plant this tree, and by planting this tree I declare that this is our land and God keeps His promises."

What are you doing in your life to proclaim that God will honor His Word? How might you be called to serve out of strength gained by the very circumstance you prayed to have removed? Believe me, I understand wishing that life was different. I wish my son were here with me right now. But I also know that God carried me through the storm of loss. And He provided me with the strength to serve from a new place of compassion and truth. My experience allows me to know firsthand and proclaim God's faithfulness. I plant my own tree in the desert by sharing my heart with you this very moment. What is your act of honor? Your proclamation for what God has brought you through? If you are in the middle of your hardest season yet, what do you hear *El Olam* promising you when you lean into His everlasting, enduring strength instead of your own temporal, human strength?

We may have been knocked out, and we may have been knocked down; things may not go the way we hope, but that should not stop us from declaring that He's true to His Word. Abraham planted a tree, and one day a tree would be God's declaration to the world of everlasting life. God's Son came and hung on a tree so that we might have life and life eternal. What are you doing practically, literally, or figuratively to declare and proclaim the power of an everlasting God regardless of the circumstances?

Faith-filled people get fueled in the waiting room. It's not like the pit stop at the racetrack, with a fast refuel and you are on your way. Though, let's face it, many people want it to be like that. We are so busy that it makes more sense to zoom in, get a quick devotional, read it in about two seconds, and be done. Then we wonder why we don't have fuel to go the long haul. If you really want your strength renewed, if you desire to mount up like an eagle, if you want to soar into the storm and beyond it instead of being blown about by it, you must learn to wait in the presence of God. You must refuel in *El Olam's* eternal Word so that you are changed in lasting ways. When you face a trial and you stumble, or an event alters your life and you are tempted to give up, you will have the everlasting source of God to draw from.

There is no quick way to get it, but you must get into His presence and allow Him to renew you through the power of His Word. If you are tempted to look elsewhere for counsel, relief, or help, ask yourself if the advice aligns with God's truth. "He who is not with

Me is against Me; and he who does not gather with Me scatters" (Matthew 12:30).

Help Comes from the Lord

I recently ran into a friend and asked how her son was. We had been praying for him because we knew he was facing a difficulty of some kind. She said, "He's struggling with addiction, but God is working on him. God's at work. I know he can be free!" Freedom is truth, freedom is life, and freedom is everlasting.

I do know this: all of my help comes from the Lord, and there are no excuses to quit. In the past I have thought, *You've got an excuse. People would give you a pass if you needed it.* But do you know what? There are no excuses; we were created for the purpose of serving and glorifying the Lord. We are to run the race that is set before us with our eyes fixed on Jesus, the author and perfector of our faith. That perfecting takes place in the waiting room.

He is *El Olam*, the Everlasting God. Beginning with faith, if you can get your arms around the reality of His character and His nature, then you can say this: "Anything that I place into the hands of Everlasting God is eternally secure." So let me ask you now, what do you need to place in the hands of everlasting God? Maybe it's your health, your spouse, your singleness, your children, your finances, or your struggles and your difficulties. Take your life and place it in the hands of Everlasting God. They are nail-scarred hands.

Those hands were nailed to a tree, the symbol of everlasting life. Ladies, nobody needs to continue carrying the burden. My challenge to you is to go to the waiting room. Ask Him, "Will You meet me there, Lord? I'll wait in Your presence. I'll listen to Your Word. I will lay my circumstances in Your hands because I trust *El Olam*. I have heard and now I know He is able to keep that which I have committed unto Him against that day."

Encountering El Olam

Trusting El Olam

1. Can you identify your waiting room experience right now? It might be something big and obvious. Or it might be a waiting that has been placed on your heart for a long time. What hope do you have that you need to entrust to *El Olam*? Trust that He, in His infinite presence and wisdom, is so much bigger than your circumstance. Know that He is beyond your limited, human understanding, and so are His answers.

2. Stop looking for solutions and start looking to *El Olam*. Take notice of how you are trying to rush along the answers or interfere with His plans because you don't want to wait. Your restlessness will decrease when you place your full trust in Him. Your temporary fixes will not be the eternal solution, so let go of your desire to control the outcome or the process getting to that outcome. Lean into His presence with faith and hope. He will not let you fall. No, not ever.

Remembering the Benefits of El Olam

1. True renewal is in short supply in the world. That is because we tend to seek it in and from the world's offerings. You are a child of the Everlasting God! There is an endless supply of nourishment and life. Go to this well when you are thirsty and hungry for abundant life. The benefits of *El Olam* are as plentiful as the stars.

2. Just as *El Olam* is limitless, so is the power He supplies to you. Look at your life in this expansive way. Can you list the limits you have placed on yourself, others, or on your circumstances? When have you said, "There is no way that person will change" or "I wish for that opportunity, but that is not possible"? Live in the limitless possibility of *El Olam*. Don't ever look at a situation or a hardened heart through your eyes again.

Blessing El Olam

1. When Abraham planted a shade tree in the desert, He proclaimed that *El Olam* keeps His promises. He honored his Lord with this act, this show of faith and gratitude. How will you honor *El Olam* for the promises fulfilled in your life? Create your own altar and offering. Plant evidence of your gratefulness and belief so the world will know He is worthy of praise.

2. The scarred hands of the Savior are reaching out to you. Are you ready to place into those hands whatever it is that burdens you and keeps you from limitless faith? Determine now what or who you are holding on to. Bless *El Olam* in His faithfulness and His patience as you pray for Him to receive that person or circumstance into His eternal hands.

Praying to El Olam

Everlasting God, I stand in awe of who You are. I confess to You that I can't even begin to get my mind around all that You represent and Your everlasting nature. Show me who You are in a very real and practical way. My past is in Your hands, my present is in Your hands, and my future is secure because I worship El Olam. *I am so grateful that I can do everything in Your limitless strength. When I stop and view my life, my pain, and my circumstances through Your eyes, I have great hope. You give me promises through Your Word and through Your actions. You are the same God of the Bible. I praise You today, Lord, and I thank You that You are the same yesterday, today, and forever. You are* El Olam. *In Jesus' name. Amen.*

9

Find Shelter in *El Elyon*

God Is Your Most High

Sometimes I lose sight of the simplicity of the truth: God is so much bigger than anything else in my life. He is bigger than anything we experience, worry about, dream up, or fight against. It should be easy to hold on to the truth that God is above all things, but I think most people forget. My hope is that together we can reinforce that certainty in our minds and hearts so that it becomes second nature—wait, let's aim for first nature—to see God as over everything and bigger than anything.

Scripture is a blessing in the pursuit of this goal because God is presented as Most High in so many different people's lives and in all kinds of circumstances and events. He is always, always reminding us that He is above everything else. He is our shelter, our coverage no matter where we go or what we face. We have the illustrations of the physical battles in Scripture to help us understand our role and our relationship to *El Elyon* in our daily spiritual battles. Those battle scenes and stories that we might be tempted to gloss over and call irrelevant are actually incredibly relevant to life now.

Each of us is standing on a battlefield. I don't know what the battle is that's going on in your life, but I am sure that you do face spiritual battles. Every believer is involved in one, whether they realize it or not. We are empowered when we realize that we are in battle. Awareness leads us to trust in God's authority for the wars we face and the skirmishes we encounter.

Blessings in the Battle

God provides us with a great example of this in Genesis 14. This chapter actually covers a 14-year time span of an ongoing physical battle. The city of Sodom, where Abram's nephew Lot lived, was captured. Their herds, their possessions, and their people were taken captive. Abram and his household army joined the fight and succeeded in throwing the enemy into confusion. They recovered all captives, along with their belongings, and returned them to their homes. After the battle, the king of Salem and the king of Sodom went out to meet and congratulate Abram. They displayed two very different attitudes toward the victory.

Salem, meaning "righteousness," was under the leadership of Melchizedek, whose name means "peace." Peace is only possible where righteousness flourishes. In Psalm 76:2, Jerusalem is referred to as Salem, the dwelling place of Mighty God. Melchizedek was the originator of the priesthood established by the Lord forever (Psalm 110:4). In the book of Hebrews, Melchizedek was the foreshadowing of the King Priest, the Lord Jesus Christ, who was designated by God as a high priest according to the order of Melchizedek.

From the earliest history of God's work and His eternal will, He was pointing toward His righteous Son, the King and Prince of Peace. He secures our peace by offering us His righteousness. Melchizedek appeared to Abram from nowhere. His parentage was not given, and no genealogy can be traced. He is eternal. He brought bread and wine as a priest of the Most High God, *El Elyon*.

He blessed Abram and acknowledged Abram's God as God Most High. They worshiped the same God and gave God Most High the glory, honor, and praise for the victory over their enemy.

Melchizedek wanted to honor Abram first and then provide a blessing. He acknowledged that Abram belonged to God Most High and then blessed *El Elyon* and Abram. And Abram, in response, honored Melchizedek and *El Elyon* by gladly tithing ten percent. When God comes to us in the battle or in the moments after, He wants us to know who we are and whose we are. He wants our identity to be clearly in Him so that we and those around us know exactly who is responsible for the victories. Abram made sure that everyone understood that he belonged to *El Elyon* and that the defeat of his enemies was God's doing.

In contrast to Melchizedek's desire to honor and bless God, the king of Sodom approached Abram with motives that were not God serving. He pretty much told Abram, "Give me the people, and I'll let you have all the stuff." Abram and God just saved this king's people, yet his thoughts were not of gratitude, they were of wealth and status. The king of Sodom represents the world. Don't we know this battle well? There is a battle between the world's agenda and God's plans. The world wants us to take and accumulate and to lift ourselves up. God calls us to trust Him for everything and to honor the King of Kings and Lord of Lords in our lives and in every battle.

Abram had revelation knowledge in that moment of the God Most High who shows up in our battles to give of Himself to bless us. No matter what you're up against in this world, you serve the One who is above, the One who is stronger, and the One who is beyond anyone or anything that comes against you.

The king of Sodom demanded more and denied God the praise and worship. That king wouldn't have even been standing there had it not been for the fact that Abram and his God came to help. Abram rescued him, but the king of Sodom demanded more. The world does this in our lives. It battles for our attention, help, affection, time, tithe, and energy. The world also wants our faith. It doesn't praise our God Most High and, instead, takes times of battle and victory to greedily grab what it doesn't deserve. And it will try to sway you to do the same.

When Abram encountered this attitude from the king of Sodom, he replied, "Oh no, I raise my hand to the God Most High." Abram did not want honor or riches; he wanted to be identified as belonging to God. He wanted to raise his hand to honor *El Elyon*.

> But Abram said to the king of Sodom, "With raised hand I have sworn an oath to the LORD, God Most High, Creator of heaven and earth, that I will accept nothing belonging to you, not even a thread or the strap of a sandal, so that you will never be able to say, 'I made Abram rich.' I will accept nothing but what my men have eaten and the share that belongs to the men who went with me." (Genesis 14:22-24 NIV)

This was his expression of worship and identity. "I belong to God. God has given me everything that I have. God meets all of my needs according to His riches in glory. I am in the care of Most High God. I want nothing that you can offer. I do not want to imply for one second that it is the world that has made me prosper."

He knew that any and all blessings, riches, and fulfilled promises came from God and God alone. Right there during a time of victory, Abram was telling everyone, "I wouldn't trade what the world can give me for the favor of God Most High."

Have you been tempted to trade away the favor of the God Most High for an offering from the world? Have you been tempted to be loyal to a cause or a position rather than to God and your identification as His? When this happens, it is because we are forgetting to raise our hand and take our oath of belief in *El Elyon*'s name, His power.

God Is Able

The experience with Melchizedek and the king of Sodom was early in Abram's walk with the Lord, and his eyes were opened to that powerful spiritual truth—the profound revelation that God was over all, above everything in his past and everything he was going to face in the future. This is the sovereignty of God. And the earlier we can learn this foundational truth, the sooner our perspective on circumstances, battles, and the world can change dramatically.

Whatever we come up against, He's in control, and He's sovereign. Have you ever found yourself lost in a spiral of thought that goes a bit like this? *Oh, this is bad. This is hard, and I don't see a way out. I don't see how this could ever change.*

Change those thoughts. Rest in the absolute truth that God is above all. When you find your mind tumbling toward defeat, take on the view of God's victory. Say to yourself, *God is above all, all the time. This circumstance didn't slip by Him. It didn't ease under a crack somewhere and get missed by His watchful eye. He's got this. My God El Elyon is over all.*

Believers are standing on a battlefield. Battles are being waged daily, and the king of Sodom is standing there in your life today as the enemy of your soul. His name is Satan, and I know that might sound radical, but it's the truth. He clothes himself as an angel of light, the Bible says, so it isn't always obvious that he is tempting you away from what is right. When he comes to offer you the goods that the world has, those offerings don't usually look blatantly wicked, threatening, or dangerous. They can even look beautiful, comfortable, easy, and well worth considering. When you stand in the presence of your king of Sodom, you might question, "Hmm, would it be so wrong to take the glory, the riches, the payoff? How do I know if this is that bad?"

You can know. You can know that what he offers will distance you from the blessing of the God Most High, because Satan's plan is to raid your home and to ravage your marriage, your business, your health, your life, and all that is dear and precious to you. Your King Melchizedek is right there too. He doesn't want you to give up what God has already secured for you on the cross. He wants you to honor what God has established. Remember, where there is righteousness, there is peace.

Nothing that happened in your past and nothing that will happen in your future is beyond God. Just as Melchizedek and *El Elyon* did for Abram after his battle, *El Elyon* does for you after each of your own battles. He blesses and nourishes you to give you life, hope, help, healing, and a future. He wants you to live in victory always.

The Spoils of God's Victory

The battle over sin in your life has been won already. God has delivered the spoils of salvation for you. What are the spoils? First of all, you're forgiven. You're clean. You're free and you're clear. Who the Son sets free is free indeed, and sin no longer has dominion over you. It doesn't have permission to rule and reign and bind and grip and hold your life down any longer.

One of the spoils of your salvation is the gift of the Holy Spirit. The Holy Spirit offers revelation knowledge and understanding and is the One who will lead you into all truth. He is the One who will give you the power to recognize the battle. The power to name the enemy. The strength to understand the strategy and to recognize when you are being drawn in by the deceptive angel of light or those who serve him. "Satan disguises himself as an angel of light. Therefore it is not surprising if his servants also disguise themselves as servants of righteousness, whose end will be according to their deeds" (2 Corinthians 11:14-15).

Those spoils of the Father, Son, and the Holy Spirit are the guarantees. They were won on the cross. That's the battle that's already been declared done, finished, and complete. And what is your response? What is your response to the kind of victory that's been given over to you? Do you live your life in humble adoration, full of the desire to honor God's victory like Abram did?

I know some modern-day Abrams. They are believers who have gone to battle. They have gone to war on behalf of other people. They have gone into the fight with prayer. They have blessed people, and God has blessed them. He's given them revelation knowledge, and He begins to use them as they prosper.

Before Abram encountered Melchizedek and the king of Sodom, God had told him of the prosperity that was part of his future. God had told Abram, "And I will make you a great nation, and I will bless you, and make your name great; and so you shall be a blessing; and I will bless those who bless you, and the one who curses you I will curse. And in you all the families of the earth will be blessed" (Genesis 12:2-4).

Even with this advance awareness of God's intentions on his life, Abram did not misinterpret the victory on behalf of Sodom as the way he was going to be great. The victory was part of his journey and part of God's plan; however, Abram understood that he was not supposed to buy into the king of Sodom's version of greatness. He did not take the advice of an ungodly man who told him to gain wealth and status. Abram knew that he was to wait for God's way to prosperity and recognition.

When faithful believers prosper in God's timing, they grow in their relationship with *El Elyon*. They recognize that they are strengthened and elevated so that they can give back and bless others. Is this the way you and I are living? Do we genuinely believe nothing we have or need comes from the world? Do we understand that the gains we experience are to be used for *El Elyon*'s service?

The spoils of our victory in Christ are plentiful. God gives you opportunities, open doors, favor, and relationships not so you can be well-known, make money, or be important or impressive, but so you can bless God with *all* of your life.

Releasing Our Hold to Give Our All

Notice that I didn't say to give to God the parts of your life that you don't want anymore. I said all of your life. This sounds so good when we are talking in our fellowship circles and when we talk to

God in private moments of prayer and supplication. However, actually giving our all can be a different story. It can be painful. There are pieces of our lives and our personalities that we tend to hold with a tight grasp.

Ask yourself, *What am I holding on to? What am I clutching to myself that really belongs to God? Is it my family, my children, my job, my resources, my talents?* I asked myself this recently. My answer? I hold tightly to my free time and my privacy. I love to be alone. Others might find that an odd thing to preserve, but I know that when I have to release my grip on that personal time, it can be a struggle. I love to be with people too, but I receive peace in my alone time. I look forward to a window of time when I know I can be on my own. So when I give from my time alone to serve or to be with people in various ways, I am giving from that free time as a tithe to God. That doesn't mean that it's easy for me. But that's the point. When we sacrifice something we hold dear so God can use it for His good, it becomes an offering to God.

What are you gripping close to your heart that is difficult for you to turn over to God Most High? Maybe your personal battle is one for control, which is a pride battle, which is a rebellion battle, which is a face-off between submitting and humbling yourself to God. What are you depending on to meet all of your needs?

Abram told the king of Sodom, an ungodly man, that he didn't even want a shoelace from the people in Sodom. He didn't want anyone else to be able to say that he got rich or famous from what the world offered. In this situation, Abram let go of worldly status and wealth and measures of both. He gave that victory to his God Most High.

Sometimes we hold on to our measures of worth or potential. Think about how much we value education in our culture. We tell our children how important it is for them to do well, to make the honor roll, and to strive for certain grades or get into good schools. Academic discipline can honor God, but we need to be sure we aren't buying into the view that there is a measure of victory other than God's good grace. While we nudge our children and ourselves to do well by the world's standards, who has been training and teaching, praying, guiding, and correcting them? Who is taking their hand and placing it in the hand of Jesus? That is our primary job. Lead them to King Jesus.

When school was rough for one of my daughters, I would tell her, "You're the top and not the bottom. You're the head and not the tail; you're the first and not the last." That's Old Testament encouragement based on Deuteronomy 28:12-14:

> The LORD will open for you His good storehouse, the heavens, to give rain to your land in its season and to bless all the work of your hand; and you shall lend to many nations, but you shall not borrow. The LORD will make you the head and not the tail, and you only will be above, and you will not be underneath, if you listen to the commandments of the LORD your God, which I charge you today, to observe them carefully, and do not turn aside from any of the words which I command you today, to the right or to the left, to go after other gods to serve them.

When I would say this, my daughter would look at me and say, "I didn't think I was the tail, Mom." That made me laugh. Even if we do not think of ourselves as either the head or the tail, the point is that when we heed God's commands, when we serve God and not the world's gods, we are able to receive from His storehouse. We will know that all blessings come from the Lord's hand, including our value and our provision.

Declaration of Dependence on God

There are sources other than God that tempt us to misplace our dependence. Are you dependent on the government for your sense of security? Are you dependent on a doctor or a lawyer to guide your next step? Are you banking on an award, a milestone, or an accomplishment to help you finally feel worthwhile?

Have you ever claimed a victory in the world's arena and then ridden the wave of self-sufficiency until an obstacle reminded you that you are completely dependent on God? Often our times of stumbling help us realize that being totally dependent on God *is* our path to total freedom, because He alone is able. Always.

We can go back to our example from Genesis for a cautionary tale. Do you know what eventually happened to the king of Sodom? God rained down fire and brimstone on all he acquired and held up as valuable. He was eliminated. All that he had in his moment of glory and time of importance that day on the battlefield and beyond was eventually no more. Sodom is remembered forever as the place that received God's wrath and judgment because the world was more important than the truth of God Most High.

Today on your battlefield, the king of Sodom is standing there and asking what more you will give him. "Will you give me the souls of your children? Will you give me your husband? Let's trade off." He wants people while you're distracted with the stuff, the pleasures, the extras, and the successes.

The entire time we're gathering the things we want and justifying how they will make life better, we are getting more and more caught up in the world's offerings. Whether we mean to or not, we are grabbing hold of the wrong thing and pledging allegiance to the world by doing so. Abram is our example. On the battlefield he proclaimed, "I'll have nothing to do with it. I won't touch it. I don't want anything you've got to offer. God Most High is my provider. You see He takes care of all of my needs. You see He leads me in victorious triumph. I will lift my hand to God Most High. I pledge my loyal service. I honor the Lord of all, the One who sits on the throne and reigns and rules forever. I give all of my life to God. I am a tithe back to God Most High." Abram was devoted to and dwelled with the Lord Most High. He knew that God alone was his shelter.

There is a rush of relief and a sense of deep peace when we fully trust where Jesus leads us and we enter the secret place of the Most High God.

Your Shelter in the Secret Place

I believe that many of the world's offerings appear to be the safe bet, at least initially. It's understandable. When we operate from a place of fear or "what if," we seek out those tangibles that ease the concern about what might happen. That's why insurance, a home, a job, a pension fund, or a five-year plan can seem like spiritual shelter. But the safe place is with God in His secret place.

> He who dwells in the secret place of the Most High
> Shall abide under the shadow of the Almighty.
> I will say of the LORD, "He is my refuge and my fortress;
> My God, in Him I will trust." (Psalm 91:1-2 NKJV)

The secret place is under the shadow of *El Elyon*. David knew of it and chose it. And I am sure that Abram knew of it and chose it over the world. You and I have the same choice. We can choose to go there to the secret place. And the way we get to the secret place is to read God's Word. This is where He speaks to us. This is where He guides us to the secret place. This is where we pitch our tents and say, "I'm not safe unless I'm under the protective covering in the secret place of the Most High God."

When we are ushered to the secret place, we discover that Jesus is the entrance. To go further, we have to let go of our agendas, demands, and versions of security. This is a gift. There is a rush of relief and a sense of deep peace when we fully trust where Jesus leads us and we enter the secret place of the Most High God. Remember, wherever you are, He's been there. He knew this was coming; He will be sufficient while you're there, and He will have victory ultimately over it all. That's your security. It can be scary to trust Jesus with your today and your tomorrow. When we encounter a trial, our minds want to look for a way out, a side door, an exit. But God needs to be our only security system. And the secret place is our eternal refuge.

When I was young, I had a friend whose mom was a really strong Christian. But I noticed that she had four deadbolt locks and an alarm system. There may have been an incident that freaked her out and stirred up her fear. But even as a young girl and a young Christian, I thought this was strange. I didn't understand why she was living like that. Yet how many of us do that? We find our own ways to feel secure, and we tend to stick to those until an encounter with the God Most High radically changes our view of His care.

Bowing Down and Looking Up

King Nebuchadnezzar thought he had it all figured out. He was secure. In fact, he was on top of the world. During his reign, he was the most important and powerful man around. At his command, the kingdom ran. He had taken Jerusalem, Israel, and Judah all into captivity. Yet a person has nothing unless the God Most High gives them favor and grants them blessing. Nebuchadnezzar had nothing in a spiritual sense. But God had planted people around him to change all that.

Those people were Daniel, Shadrach, Meshach, and Abednego. These were Jewish men who were taken captive. And while some might assume that they were mere prisoners who could affect no change and wield no influence, we know that *El Elyon* can do anything through anyone in any circumstance—even those that seem impossible. God's people are not limited by circumstances, because God can reach into any place, no matter how dark, and reveal His power and light. All He has to do is open the door for His people to impact others.

God had His people ready and waiting to speak truth into Nebuchadnezzar's life. When the king couldn't get anyone in his circle to effectively interpret his dreams, he was angry. With all his earthly power and might, he was the one who was limited. Then he called on Daniel, one of God's people, to reveal the truth of his dreams. Daniel, who gave credit to God for the discernment and wisdom he shared with the king, bravely shared with Nebuchadnezzar that one of his dreams foretold his pending fall from power. This fall did come to pass, and it was so significant that the man who was once king lived like an animal in the wild for a period of time. And, just as the dream also prophesied, Nebuchadnezzar turned his heart and eyes to Daniel's God. " 'But at the end of that period, I, Nebuchadnezzar, raised my eyes toward heaven and my reason returned to me, and I blessed the Most High and praised and honored Him who lives forever' " (Daniel 4:34).

What was Nebuchadnezzar's response when he looked up? He said he saw the Most High and he praised Him and he honored Him. This man who was immersed in his own power and who looked only at the wealth and influence of the world suddenly had eyes to see the Lord. He proclaimed that the Most High lives forever. Nebuchadnezzar got a glimpse of reality. His dominion would end, but God's dominion is forever and ever.

Look up, Friend. If you feel like your life has been reduced, confined, or limited, look up. If you have lost everything that at one time made you feel important, look up. If you lost the one person who made you feel valued and safe, look up. Fix your eyes on *El Elyon*. He sees you in your circumstance, but He does not see limitations; He sees the potential for His will to be done and for His name to be praised.

When we look up, something transforming happens. We stop asking God to come down and to enter our world, and we start seeking the way of God Most High. God is called the lifter of your head because when He lifts your head, you look up. And when you look up you see Him high and lifted up, seated on the throne in His glory and with His might. Your redemption is near, and you don't want to be looking down and miss seeing His arrival and His purposes unfolding.

When you and I give our all to God, our perspective does change. We realize that our circumstances, battles, fears, anxieties, sorrows, losses, sicknesses, and threats to our security are all under the sovereign care of God Most High.

So wherever you stand today, whatever your personal battle is, turn your eyes to Him and say with absolute assurance, "Shall not the God of all the earth do what is right in my circumstances, in my situation? I bow my knee and I give all of myself to You."

Encountering El Elyon

Trusting El Elyon

1. When have you encountered a king of Sodom? In what ways have the world's offerings been a temptation for you either in the past or in your life now? Consider how different it feels to spend time with a Melchizedek who will bless you and draw your focus back to the Lord.

2. Abram strongly expressed his conviction that he served *El Elyon* and belonged to the God Most High. Find a way this week to proclaim your identity in *El Elyon*. Stating your faith can be scary at first, but you will discover that God is right there with you. You will draw near to God Most High when you honor Him with your actions and words. Your declaration of identity in Christ will help another person see *El Elyon* in their own life.

Remembering the Benefits of El Elyon

1. Which of the spoils of God's victory have you experienced? When you lean into the revelation and understanding of God and the Holy Spirit living within, you will walk, talk, act, pray, and love others as a woman who has been freed through salvation instead of as a woman who is still captive. Remember the benefits of Christ's victory because they do not fade away. You have access to them for your life. And just imagine all that *El Elyon* can do through you when you fully embrace those spoils as a humble victor.

2. *El Elyon* is your refuge and fortress. You need not find a

substitution for Him in the world. Your security, measure of value, and deepest need can be brought into the secret place of the Most High. Seek the secret place through His Word. Enter the secret place through the sacrifice and grace of Christ.

Blessing El Elyon

1. Nebuchadnezzar had it all and then lost it. At the end of that ordeal, he wasn't bitter but was led to look upward, to cast his eyes on the God Most High. When have you experienced a loss so great that the world's offerings were no longer a comfort? When did you encounter the bottom of the pit? Has that experience hardened your heart, or has it opened it up? Look to *El Elyon* today. Daniel's God is your God. Release bitterness and look up at Him.

2. Bless *El Elyon* now by prayerfully lifting up that past pain to Him as you also lift your eyes to see and honor Him. Give Him the very thing that caused you pain as a way to bless Him. When you become open to God using your darkest times for His good purposes, your healing will bless Him and bless those that *El Elyon* brings into your life. Consider how you also might be a Daniel to another person, always guiding them back to the revelation of God. Always trust that there is not any circumstance that *El Elyon* is not over. And there is no pain or disappointment too great for Him to redeem.

Praying to El Elyon

El Elyon, *I come into Your presence and I'm humbled all over again. You are my God, and You are awesome in power. Lord, forgive me for the many times I have forgotten who You are and I have neglected to look up and to remember my God is higher than any other. I get stuck in my life because I rely on my limited perspective of what matters and what can be done. But You are beyond those human, fearful boundaries. There is nothing that You cannot do. Help me to rest in this every single day.*

Open my eyes to the revelation of who You are, El Elyon, *God Most High, so that I see You seated above the mess and beauty of life. You are above my fears. You are above my enemies. You are above my doubts. You are above my battles. I give to You my life, my all. All of my concerns, failures, pride, and victories are lifted up today in Your presence,* El Elyon. *May my words and actions glorify You each day. In Jesus' name. Amen.*

10

Serve Faithfully with *Adonai*

God Is Your Lord and Master

I prayed about which of God's names we would close with together. It came to me that *Adonai*, meaning "Lord and Master," was an ideal choice. It is a little different from the other names. Those we've explored help us see who God is, and they help us see what He does for our lives and us. *Adonai*, however, speaks of something broader than a characteristic or an attribute of God. Understanding God as Lord and Master deepens our understanding of relationship *with* God. If all of these names don't lead us into a relationship, it's really just a lot of information.

Desperate to Be His

We belong to *Adonai*. He is our Master, and it's a privilege to be His possession. I'm thankful and humbled to be the property of *Adonai*. In fact, if I don't belong to Him, I don't have life. I have come to a place where I understand how desperate I am to belong to Him and to be His possession.

Are you in that place too? Have circumstances or a deepening need in your life drawn you to the feet of the Master? As servants, we surrender absolute control and complete rule over our every breath, action, thought, and dream to Him. It is easy to talk about this hypothetically; however, it can be difficult to live out a wholly surrendered existence. In my life, I know that if I am going to be in relationship with *Adonai*, I need to embrace the truth that my family and home are not mine. My finances aren't mine. My health isn't mine. My abilities or inabilities are not my own. God's my Master, and whatever He's given to me belongs to Him.

How scary is that to you right now? When you make your own list, which of your possessions, priorities, people, or hopes are the most difficult to give over to Him? Which do you hold on to with desperation, believing it is best to keep it under your control? The truth is, we aren't giving to God what is ours to begin with. Everything originates with Him! And He has paid a great price.

God is worthy of our everything because our salvation cost Him everything.

Why We Surrender All

The Bible tells us, "You were bought with a price" (1 Corinthians 7:23). It cost Him everything He had to purchase our redemption. He set the example and showed us the standard for our relationship with and to Him.

> Have this attitude in yourselves which was also in Christ Jesus, who, although He existed in the form of God, did not regard equality with God a thing to be grasped, but emptied Himself, taking the form of a bond-servant, and being made in the likeness of men. Being found in appearance as a man, He humbled Himself by becoming obedient to the point of death, even death on a cross. (Philippians 2:5-8)

The Lord of glory, the King of heaven, the name that is above every name lowered Himself to be in the likeness of men. He suffered and was obedient to a cross. In turn, obedience, suffering, and surrender are what it costs us to have Him as Master. It is backward from the world's way. If you tell someone that you are aiming for success via humble servanthood, they will think you've gone off the deep end. Instead, you have dived into the deep end of commitment to your Lord and *His* glory.

The most precious thing I've learned in becoming a servant is that my Master takes full responsibility for me. He's responsible for protecting, providing, guiding, and leading me every step of the way. I don't have to figure everything out. Ah. Let that sink in. I encourage you to speak aloud the following sentences several times until they resonate with your soul and your reasoning mind. *As Adonai's servant, I don't have to figure everything out. He takes full charge and full responsibility of me.* Can you identify with that game-changing freedom? When we are servants of *Adonai*, we discover we have never been so free.

I don't have to worry. I don't have to plan. I don't have to control. I don't have to try to hang on to—or earn—the pieces of life that the world deems valuable. My Master has pledged Himself to me, and I can trust His capable hands.

In *Adonai* We Are Fearless

God takes the well-being of all those that are in His household very seriously. He protects us. "But You, O LORD, are a shield about me, my glory, and the One who lifts my head" (Psalm 3:3). We can trust and know that we are hidden in Christ even when we are downcast or fear attacks us. Are you afraid today? Is it possible that today's fears are rooted in your past?

What has come to pass can imbed fear in our hearts and minds. Do you relive the past accompanied by anxious thoughts? *What if someone finds out? I can't let go of how much I have been hurt. How can I move forward when my past haunts me?*

Or are you afraid of your future unknowns?

People might not even realize that they are frozen with fear, but you can hear it in what surfaces in conversation. "I don't know how I will go on from here. What if things change for the worse? I don't know what our family's provision status will be next year. Can I trust this person to come through for me? I don't know how to go forward with a broken heart." Maybe you have said some of these things too?

There is peace ahead for you. When you place yourself as *Adonai's* servant, your Master is fully responsible for you, including your past and your future. He will be responsible for your well-being physically, emotionally, and spiritually. When you can't see an answer, when you can't find a trace of evidence to justify your faith, hang on to His Word and seek *Adonai's* reign over your life.

We view surrender as a restriction, a lessening. God views surrender as an invitation to experience the highest calling we can ever have: to serve *Adonai*.

The past or the future woe that keeps you up at night, that is all His too. But you must first embrace the position of servant. Let your heart cry, "Without You, Lord, I can't go forward! I know I need You; I have neglected Your Word, but I'm back, Lord. I trust You with everything." He honors such faith.

Less Is More in the Lord

God's instructions make no room for misunderstanding. In Matthew 6, Jesus says straight out that you cannot serve two masters; you will love one and hate the other. You will be loyal to one and despise the other. He sums it all up: you cannot serve God and man.

You cannot serve God and this world. Too often we find ourselves in conflict because we are trying to serve two masters, if not *multiple* masters. Our loyalties are divided between masters of money, recognition and status, physical beauty, the illusion of security, etc. If we are distracted with our own world of plans and preparations, we will not be able to hear the Master's voice when He comes to call, and we will not be ready to walk in the way the Master leads.

When you release yourself from the service of other masters, you will be liberated from their entanglements and distraction. You can focus on the Lord, await the Master's biding, and rise to your calling in Christ. He will speak to you through His Word, His Holy Spirit, other believers, and prayer. Be alert. Watch, listen, look. Then serve with gladness.

The Joys of Servanthood

I believe that people want Christ to be Savior, but they aren't so sure about this requirement of making Him Lord. Does a small part of you worry about what making Him Lord will require? The sin nature resists submitting and surrendering our personal rights. "I'm going to have to give up…I'm going to have to quit…I'm going to have to let go of…I won't be able to…!"

We view surrender as a restriction, a lessening. God views surrender as an invitation to experience the highest calling we can ever have: to serve *Adonai*. He wants us to know freedom and joy. He wants us to have abundant life that emerges when we are free of what the world puts before us to distract us. Let's take in the full joy of servanthood. We are gaining Christ by leaving behind allegiance to the world's standards. David expresses this in such a simple, profound way. "Preserve me, O God, for I take refuge in You. I said to the LORD, 'You are my LORD; I have no good besides You'" (Psalm 16:1-2).

As we take refuge in *Adonai*'s care and kingdom, it becomes clear that there is no good thing apart from Him. Nothing. When we grip tightly to the outcome of an investment of time and energy, we are holding on to something less than God's good plan that leads to the ultimate good: eternal life. "But now having been freed from sin and enslaved to God, you derive your benefit, resulting in sanctification, and the outcome, eternal life. For the wages of sin is death, but the free gift of God is eternal life in Christ Jesus our Lord" (Romans 6:22-23).

The benefits of being under *Adonai* are many: holiness, righteousness, sanctification, and life everlasting. That's freedom! When you're shackled by sin, bound by your past, and handcuffed to guilt and shame, you are enslaved to the enemy. The wages of sin is death. The devil makes you pay, but the eternal gift of God is just that—a free gift and a *freeing* gift.

Following the Master's Lead

Jesus says, "I have so much more for you." If we want to know the benefits of our relationship to *Adonai*, then we must do as He has done. "I gave you an example that you also should do as I did to you. Truly, truly, I say to you, a slave is not greater than his master, nor is one who is sent greater than the one who sent him. If you know these things, you are blessed if you do them" (John 13:15-17).

Do you know what Jesus was doing when He made that statement? He was washing the filthy, smelly feet of His disciples. They had gone ahead and secured an upper room in which to share a last meal together to celebrate the Passover. Jesus noticed that there was not a servant present, and it was against custom to recline at the table with dirty feet. It was a servant's job, the houseman's job, to wash the feet of the guests at the table. Did He assign the humbling task to one of the disciples to teach a lesson? No. Instead, Jesus stood up, took off His robe, and wrapped Himself with a towel. He knelt down with a basin of water, and He showed the disciples that there was nothing in them that was too stinky, too dirty, or too ugly to be tended to by the Lord. He came to serve and to humble Himself, and He instructed us to do the same.

When was the last time you lowered yourself to minister to someone who was offensive or difficult? Have you ever found that serving with a right attitude is most demanding at home and with the people you love? We don't want to strip away the way we are viewed in order to be vulnerable and openhearted. It is painful to do so. Can you think of a time when you broke through that fear of pain and openness? Did you bow your pride and resistance so you could minister with kindness? It isn't easy to put ourselves aside to be fully present and completely humbled before another person.

Not long ago I was trying to embrace this particular lesson. I was asking God to show me what this would look like in my life situation. I no longer have any children at home making the demands that children make. I wasn't dealing with anyone particularly difficult in my daily interactions. So how was I supposed to fully experience this lesson? Then one night, my husband came home and asked if I could attend an event with him that evening. There it was, my chance to bow down and graciously express a servant's heart. In my mind, my first response was a selfish line of thought: "Are you kidding me? I have a life too, you know. That's your kind of thing." Then it struck me that this was my invitation to act from a servant's heart of love and put myself aside. Where is God calling you to simply bow and say, "I will do this because it's as if Jesus Himself has asked me to"? He gives of Himself with no expectations in return and without a mental storm of divisive, selfish thoughts before He serves.

We have so much to learn about how to do as Christ did and does. I praise *Adonai* for His eternal patience. When He should be fed up with me, He continues to wait. He continues to come back one more time and say, "Let Me wash that dirt away. Let Me take care of it for you."

Imitating Christ in Real Life

Imagine gathering your friends and family around your dining table and asking them to honestly share how or *if* your life imitates that of Jesus. "I just need an honest answer—I'm really trying to grow. Do you see anything in me that reminds you of Jesus?"

Serving in the world is all about qualifications, recognition, rewards, being called out, being called up, being exalted, and letting everybody know and everybody see. Serving in the kingdom is all about dying to self, suffering, and emptying. We are to be vessels of God's love and compassion and to be His touch to the untouchable. What we have to ask ourselves is, "How serious am I about serving Jesus?" Do we want our name on a program? Do we want to be recognized by the public? Or do we want to be a servant, knowing that it means we will experience pain and sacrifice without recognition for it?

Think about how invisible servants are when they are part of a royal household. We've seen shows, we've read books; we know that servants are to serve and slip away. They aren't praised when they are bowed down, humbled, and doing their job. When we serve *Adonai*, we will do much behind the scenes and without the accolades we might have longed for in the past.

Do you want to go into the prayer closet alone? Will you step up to do the work of God that nobody knows about? Do you want to truly be like Jesus? Because it will cost. It isn't impossible even if we might initially feel like it is. Why is it that we are prone to think that total surrender and humility is just for super-Christians, the unsung rock stars of the faith? This false belief can temporarily make us feel better when we stumble in our commitment. *No wonder this isn't working—I'm not one of the incredible Christians, those saints who walk the earth. I'm a regular believer. I won't ever match their humility, so why even try?* Well, we try and we do because *Adonai* asks us to. Because God is our Master and Christ bought us with a price.

The bargain is ours, my friend. He paid the price, and we receive the privilege of serving. It doesn't stop there. We have the privilege of serving, and we have the *power* of the Master to serve. You and I are not abandoned to find our own way to serve. God is with us to provide the strength and the means just as He was for Jesus, the holy Servant.

> "Behold, My Servant, whom I uphold;
> My chosen one in whom My soul delights.
> I have put My Spirit upon Him;
> He will bring forth justice to the nations." (Isaiah 42:1)

This verse really makes me think about our relationship with God. When we bow our knee to *Adonai*, we can say, "I am Your servant, Lord. You are Master, and You promise to uphold me. That is your part." The Holy Spirit lives in us so that we too have the power of Christ to bring justice and truth to a lost and dying world.

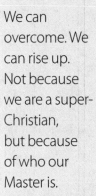

We can overcome. We can rise up. Not because we are a super-Christian, but because of who our Master is.

Asking the Master Your Questions

How do we walk in this power? How do we know where to go? These are the questions that plague us in the daily trenches of caring for our families, driving the carpool, juggling job responsibilities, and volunteering for the local shelter. Even when our hearts and minds are aligned with the desire to serve *Adonai*, we will need to know how to move forward in obedience. We will see assurance from our Lord.

Do you ever have those nights when your family is fast asleep but you are wide-awake with a storm of questions whirling about your mind? What overwhelming questions have kept you awake lately? I am often wondering what is next and whether I am being faithful in what *Adonai* wants for me and from me.

We aren't the only ones with questions. Scripture is filled with the questions that rise up from God's many servants. See, even the champions of our faith were not "super-Christians," not by a long shot. They questioned. They doubted. In fact, the very first time God is addressed as *Adonai* in the Bible, it is when Abram is asking more questions, even as he is submitting.

When Abram had still not fathered a child, God's promise seemed more and more unlikely. After God reinforced His faithfulness by saying, "Do not fear, Abram, I am a shield to you; your reward shall be very great" (Genesis 15:1), Abram still felt compelled to ask again about God's promise and plan. He wasn't being difficult; he was actually doing his best to be faithful and steadfast when he called on *Adonai*. " 'O Lord God, what will You give me, since I am childless, and the heir of my house is Eliezer of Damascus?' And Abram said, 'Since You have given no offspring to me, one born in my house is my heir' " (Genesis 15:2-3).

It's as if he is saying, "Um, God there doesn't seem to be an answer yet. Did You come up with a new plan?" As we explored in earlier chapters, Abram was discouraged when the promise of fathering future generations was not yet unfolding. While his family and people and herds slept, his mind was likely reeling with questions: "Where's that great nation, Lord? Where's the great name? What about that descendant, God?" Abram wasn't trying to be difficult. I truly believe that he was stepping up in faith and saying, "All I want, Lord, is what You alone can give. So tell me if anything has changed; I don't want anything that is not of You."

Abram called on his Lord and Master as an act of submission. And God honored this act. God did not get testy over Abram's questions. Instead, He lovingly reassured His servant. "This man will not be your heir; but one who will come forth from your own body, he shall be your heir" (Genesis 15:4). Abram's fear was put to rest. He was encouraged to stay true to the path and promise of the Master. Eventually he saw his Master's promise fulfilled.

If we can do the same when those questions jolt us awake or create a ruckus in the back of our mind and spirit while we go about our day, we will be able to let go of the fear-based questions. It is fine to have questions, but we must understand that those questions, if not given over to God, will eventually become the obstacles between us and God's calling for us. However, if we speak our concerns and then ultimately submit to and even long for what God alone can give, we will be used by the Master. Trust will replace the fear.

Maybe the desire of your heart is to have a husband. Maybe you long to have a child or a grandchild. In this season of your life, maybe you are waiting for a ministry to unfold, and you're thinking, like Abram did, that the promise God gave you is not happening. It is not on the horizon. But if God gave you a word, hold on to that word! Don't settle for anything less.

Adonai's Question for Your Life

Knowing God deeply and personally is the greatest joy and blessing we will experience during our time on earth and in heaven. This is our most noble, worthwhile, urgent pursuit. This allows us to listen for His voice and His command with our spiritual ears. When we do, we will hear the important question *Adonai* has for you and me. It comes to us through Scripture, and it will come to our minds and hearts in that crucial moment of God's calling on our lives. "Then I heard the voice of the Lord, saying, 'Whom shall I send, and who will go for Us?'" (Isaiah 6:8).

Isaiah's beloved Master wanted to know if he would follow Him. This was Isaiah's commission. This is the question that we will encounter during different seasons of our life. When we serve God, we are to be expectant of such a question and then respond with a servant's surrendered, committed heart. Isaiah did that very thing when he responded, "Here am I. Send me!"

That is a servant. We could not have a better example of a prepared servant's heart. God was calling Isaiah to a very difficult trial. He called him to be a prophet who would bear difficult news to sinners and would watch them fall to ruin. But Isaiah was asked by his Master. And he responded with a ready servant's heart. He was prepared and in position to be called. Knowing God by name is not only about strengthening our relationship with the Lord and building our faith, but it is also about being tuned in to Him so we hear Him call us to service.

The Way Is Clear—Walk in It

Are you in position to be called? Have you been struck by your need and surrendered to Christ? If you've seen the Lord for who He is and you see yourself for who you are, would you trust that obedience is the only requirement for provision? Remember it's the Master's job to provide for your needs and the needs of your commission. The Master's not going to send a servant who cannot do what He calls him to do. I know we hear that all the time, but I just want to tell you because you might be standing before God today saying, "I don't know if I have time. I don't know if I have enough Bible knowledge. I don't know if I have the skills. I don't know if I can do that."

꧁꧂꧁꧂꧁꧂

It is a joyful moment in our lives when we call
out to *Adonai* and say, "Make me ready and
willing to hear Your call."

Look to, rely on, lean on, and lean into the Master. Hold on to the truth and promise we gathered from our time getting to know the Shepherd. This verse bears repeating and memorizing. "Now the God of peace, who brought up from the dead the great Shepherd of the sheep through the blood of the eternal covenant, even Jesus our Lord, equip you in every good thing to do His will, working in us that which is pleasing in His sight, through Jesus Christ" (Hebrews 13:20-21).

The "who am I" questions can be a challenge unless we hold to the promise of this verse. You know—those questions that are about your lack rather than God's greatness. "Oh, Jesus, who am I that You would call me forward in Your will for Your great purposes? I have no qualifications. I am a flawed human. Who am I that You would give me the privilege to hold up the Word of Life? Who am I that You would let me be a mom? Who am I that You would give me a husband as a protecting cover? Who am I that You would consider me for a position of leadership or influence? Who am I...?" If God calls you, you can do it. If God calls you, He equips you.

The answer is, you are *Adonai's* child. You are the servant to your faithful Lord and Master. I want to assure you that He makes a way. He will clear the path so that steps forward can be taken. Does this mean the road will be trouble free? Absolutely not. But it does mean that God has gone before and the Master who beckons you to rise up and answer His call will also be the Creator, All-Sufficient One, Provider, Healer, Banner, Peace, Shepherd, Everlasting, and Most High who will accompany you and strengthen you for what you will face.

If there seem to be too many options and crossroads ahead, know that God will narrow your focus. In fact, this narrowing and enabling can be one of your assurances that something is from the Lord. "Not that we are adequate in ourselves to consider anything as coming from ourselves, but our adequacy is from God" (2 Corinthians 3:5).

Adonai will begin to delete things from your life that don't matter.

He will strengthen and add in areas that *do* matter. Before too long, you will not even remember old priorities or insecurities. It is a joyful moment in our lives when we call out to *Adonai* and say, "Make me ready and willing to hear Your call."

When you hear the call, you can know the way by looking to Him.

> Behold, as the eyes of servants look to the hand of
> their master,
> As the eyes of a maid to the hand of her mistress,
> So our eyes look to the Lord our God,
> Until He is gracious to us. (Psalm 123:2)

When God entrusts you with a calling, a commission, He is asking you to honor Him with your choices moving forward. In Matthew, Jesus' parable of the talents revealed the price and the prize of doing so with integrity and faith. There was a master who, before leaving on a long journey, gave to one of his servants five talents, which is a measure of money. He gave another servant two talents. And he gave the third servant one talent. The first two servants doubled their money in the master's absence. But the third servant buried his single talent and earned no return. He didn't have faith. His fear led him to bury it, to stop the potential of blessing and serving the master. To the ones who came back and gave more, the master said, "Well done, good and faithful slave. You were faithful with a few things. I will put you in charge of many things; enter into the joy of your master" (Matthew 25:21). When we, as God's servants, fearlessly use what our Master gives to us, we shall reap an abundance that pleases Him.

You have a treasure. God has invested in you by depositing a treasure of truth in your heart. He has entrusted you with spiritual wealth. Now it is your turn to trust Him. I can't encourage you enough to trust Him and to listen for His call. It may be to serve a small neighborhood group, class, or a friend. It may be to return to your church or lead a prayer group. I don't know what it is, but I do know that you shouldn't depend on someone else. You are the one to account for what you do with anything *Adonai* places on your heart and in your care. Take it, surrender it back, and say, "Master, I'm here to serve You. I want to hear You say, 'Well done, good and faithful servant.'"

Encountering Adonai

Trusting Adonai

1. What about the past or the future concerns you most? These worries, sins, and experiences belong to *Adonai*. Humble your spirit today as you surrender these to God. How does this affect your outlook? How might this peace change the way you approach each new day?

2. Determine which worldly master has been your biggest entanglement and distraction. How long has this kept you from submitting to God as Master? Consider which practical steps you can take to detach your allegiance.

Remembering the Benefits of Adonai

1. The benefit of surrendering to *Adonai* is that you are not in control! How does falling back into the hands of your Master free you? Which burdens have weighed heaviest on your heart? Consider how the relinquishing of these will change your outlook, ability to serve, and spiritual peace.

2. God has entrusted to you, His servant, treasures of the heart and soul. What do you sense them to be? Think of three ways to invest them faithfully so that you experience the reward of honoring the Master with the fruit of submission.

Blessing Adonai

1. If you, like Abram, have not yet seen God's promises fulfilled, bless Him today as you present your questions. Then, with

sincerity and submission, reinforce your surrender to Him as *Adonai* in your life.

2. You bless *Adonai* when you are patient and attentive. In this space of submission, you can hear His call. How has your Master been leading you through His Word, voice, and other faithful servants? Pray about this calling and seek His guidance for your next steps.

Praying to Adonai

Master, I thank You for the most precious relationship that has been formed, this relationship between Adonai *and me, Your servant. What a privilege, what a joy, what an honor it is to belong to You. I am so grateful that You made each and every one who calls on the name of Jesus Your servant. I pray to be patient as I train my heart to hear You and receive Your call to serve. I want to release my questions to You now so that I replace any doubt with the freeing peace of certainty in my Master's plan and power. May I look up to You and see Your mercy as You give to me a treasure to use and multiply for Your glory. When I see You face to face, may it be so that You can say, "Well done. Well done, good and faithful servant." I am Yours, Lord. All that I am and have is from Your hand. I surrender it all back to You so that You can shape my days, hone my priorities, and guide my feet on this path of life and purpose. I fall to my knees with a humble spirit. It is a privilege to serve my gracious, all-powerful, all-loving* Adonai. *In Jesus' name I pray. Amen.*

Acknowledgments

To my husband, Frank, and my daughters, Morgan, Caroline, and Carter. Each of you has faithfully prayed, pushed, and prodded when I doubted myself and offered generous praise to encourage me every step of the way. I love you more than you can ever know.

To each woman who attended Women of the World Bible Study in Charlotte, North Carolina. Thank you for sharing your thoughts and revelations with each other and with me.

This study was originally created the year following James's death. Through the support of Margaret, Jackie, Katie, and especially the small group leadership, I was freed to grieve, and you enabled me to begin healing. Your love and prayer allowed me to return and find strength and courage, one baby step at a time. You hold in your hands the fruit of what seemed like a barren period in my life.

To Robert Walker, who first sowed the seed of possibility that God wanted to do more through me. You continue to challenge and inspire me to remember that God uses all things that we surrender to Him.

To my team at Stepping Toward Hope, especially Savanna, Sarah, Nadia, and Steve. Without you, this book would not have reached completion. Thanks for the fun we have had along the way.

To Bob Hawkins Jr., LaRae Weikert, Hope Lyda, and the supportive Harvest House team. Thank you for helping me find my voice and honoring my message. Your care and patience have set me on an amazing journey that has allowed me to share what God has placed on my heart.

Last, but not least, to my prayer team. Anything of eternal value begins in prayer. This message is credited to your account in heaven.

About the Author

Jan Harrison has been inspiring women for more than 20 years as a Bible teacher and speaker at women's conferences and retreats. She served on the leadership committee for Anne Graham Lotz's *Just Give Me Jesus* revivals.

She wrote *Life After the Storm* to share how the unexpected death of her son transformed her life and tested her faith, and to offer readers hope and the tools to experience the transforming faith that only a storm can unveil. She shares *Becoming a Woman Who Knows God by Name* to encourage women to lean on the strength of God's character for their every need and to live out the benefits of His character in their lives.

In late 2015, Jan created Stepping Toward Hope, a platform that exists to empower individuals to embrace peace, strength, and comfort in Christ by encouraging everyone to be equipped with His Word. Her desire to minister hope to other people continues to flow from her heart.

Jan and her husband, Frank, live in Charlotte, North Carolina. They are involved in the local and global faith community and are leaders in an international ministry, With Open Eyes, founded by their late son, James F. Harrison IV. They have three grown daughters and three grandchildren.

For more information or to contact Jan for a speaking engagement, visit www.steppingtowardhope.org.

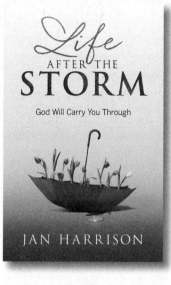

Are winds of change, doubt, or grief swirling around you?

Engaging author and teacher Jan Harrison shares how, when storms strike, you can depend on God's spiritual supplies—His promises, His Spirit, His ever-present help, and the treasures of His Word.

After a storm of loss forever changed the landscape of Jan's life, her faith and years of Bible study were tested. In that journey, she discovered how God was and is able to fill her every need. Now, with compassion and courage, Jan will help you:

* stop living in fear of "what if" and be ready for life "even if"

* sense God's constant presence and gentle healing

* experience the transforming confidence and faith that only a storm can unveil

Whether you or someone you care about faces a difficult season, the lifelines of God's promises will lead you to life and hope after the storm.

Stepping Toward Hope
Moving Through Your Storm
with Jan Harrison

Stepping Toward Hope with Jan Harrison empowers individuals to embrace peace, strength and comfort in Christ by encouraging everyone to be equipped with His word.

SteppingTowardHope.org

 /OfficialJanHarrison

 @JanHarrison_STH

 @JanHarrison_STH